Recordings:
A Select Bibliography of Contemporary African,
Afro-Caribbean and Asian British Art
Institute of International Visual Arts and
Chelsea College of Art and Design, London 1996
Written and Compiled by Melanie Keen and
Elizabeth Ward

Acknowledgements

Published by the Institute of International Visual Arts (inIVA) in collaboration with Chelsea College of Art and Design, 1996

Copyright © the Institute of International Visual Arts (inIVA) and Chelsea College of Art and Design, 1996

Institute of International Visual Arts
Kirkman House
12/14 Whitfield Street
London W1P 5RD

ISBN 1 899846 06 9
A catalogue record for this book is available from the British Library.

Compiled and written by Melanie Keen and Liz Ward
Design: 8vo, London
Printed in the UK by G&B Printers, Middlesex

institute of international visual arts

Funded by THE ARTS COUNCIL OF ENGLAND

LONDON ARTS BOARD

This publication would not have been possible without the work of Elizabeth Ward who created the archive at Chelsea and the previous in-house editions of this bibliography. The research project was generously funded by The London Institute and I am grateful for the support of Bridget Jackson, Head of Chelsea College of Art and Design. I hope this publication bears eloquent testimony to the quiet efficiency, knowledge and skills of our research assistant, Melanie Keen: she was supported again by Elizabeth Ward, and my other colleagues, Donald Smith, Vicky Webb and Stacy Billups, who tragically died before this enterprise was fulfilled.

To Eddie Chambers, for generous donations of materials and stimulating feedback, we owe particular thanks. We are grateful for the help of the following individuals and organisations: Eileen Daly; Mark Segal (The Cut Gallery); Lydia Yee (The Bronx Museum of the Arts, New York); Steve McIntyre (London Film and Video Development Agency); The Street Level Gallery, Glasgow; Paul Bayley (Cornerhouse, Manchester); Caroline Harris (The October Gallery, London); The 198 Gallery, London; The Worcester Museum and Art Gallery, Worcestershire; Josephine Ryan, Clare Hungate and Catherine Ugwu (The Institute of Contemporary Arts, London); The Whitechapel Art Gallery, London; Sankofa; The Brixton Art Gallery, London; The Rochdale Art Gallery, Rochdale; The Lisson Gallery, London; Bluecoat Gallery, Liverpool; Shaheen Merali & Panchayat; Jeremy Theophilus; The Islington Arts Factory, London; Mappin Art Gallery, Sheffield; Zarina Bhimji; Sutapa Biswas; Sonia Boyce; Gavin Jantjes; Danny Padmore; Alistair Raphael; Julian Richards; Robert Saunders; AAVAA; Camerawork, London; Focal Point Gallery, Southend; The Ikon Gallery, Birmingham, and all the individuals and organisations who have contributed to this project over the years.

Because this bibliography reflects the collection at Chelsea, it will have gaps, and we would encourage anyone to send us items for inclusion in future editions.

The single most important stage in the development of an artist's practice is arguably having their work exhibited and subsequently documented in some form so that it stakes a claim for recognition in the world. Only by having support structures in place, such as a sympathetic curator and/or writer with provisory space, can an artist expect to realise this goal. This has been particularly true of work made by artists who are of African, Afro-Caribbean and Asian descent.(1) However, each artists' story unfolds with varying degrees of acceptance, exclusion and finally recognition. Within Recordings, a document of documents, those stories reveal themselves by whom and what have been documented, written about and subsequently published.

Documenting the work of black artists practising in Britain has sometimes been 'do-it-yourself' in nature. Some earlier catalogues, produced as xerox copies, reflect the resourceful character of individual artists and the firm hope that their document would be collected. On another level, the notion of DIY practice refers more profoundly to taking the initiative and being able to recognise a gap in the range of books that deal with contemporary art practice; when there was no one there to do it for you, you would do-it-yourself. As time has passed, catalogues have changed in their appearance – they are more sophisticated now in terms of the print technology and materials used to produce them, mainly because of the money made available that helped fund the production. When publishing these catalogues and books, how could the 'producer' be certain that they would be collected? The fact is that many art libraries in Britain are poor resources for those researching not only contemporary black British artists, but artists from a plurality of cultures.(2)

Library users often have to demand that these documents are collected, but these demands are not always heard. The archive which has fed into Recordings was established in 1985 at the St. Martin's School of Art library, before it became part of the London Institute. Establishing the archive was the result of demands made by black students for documentation that recognised the contributions made to British art by their contemporaries and predecessors. Also new directives on multi-cultural education introduced by the ILEA – the now defunct Inner London Education Authority – affected the development of this resource. Having supportive and sympathetic librarians ensured that the archive grew and found a permanent home at Chelsea School of Art once the London Institute was formed. This is not to say that the responsibility of collecting rests firmly at Chelsea's library door. While there are other organisations such as the African and Asian Visual Artists Archive (AAVAA) and the library at The Institute of International Visual Arts (inIVA) who are collecting widely and systematically, it does not mean that the onus remains on either or all of these collectors. Other institutions need to re-evaluate their own collections and this bibliography can assist them in that task.

Recordings is separated into three main sections plus an index: a chronology, a list of individual artists and general texts. The chronology has recorded, as comprehensively as the availability of material has allowed, group exhibitions that black artists participated in from 1971 to early 1996, with accompanying reviews and articles. Earlier documentation about first-generation Afro-Caribbean artists have been recorded in Anne Walmsley's invaluable book The Caribbean Artists Movement 1966 – 1972: A Literary and Cultural History. On the whole, printed matter promoting this work has consisted of theme-based group shows: a predominance of these appeared in the 1980s. By the same token, there were exhibitions that centred on the geographical location of the artist, such as Caribbean Expressions in Britain (1986) or the medium of their practice, for example Sculptors' Drawings (1994).

In the 1960s and 1970s, the exhibition spaces that were dedicated to showing black artists were either the Commonwealth Institute, the Africa Centre and DRUM Arts Centre in London. The emergence of spaces and organisations in the 1980s, such as the Black Art Gallery, the Horizon Gallery, the 198 Gallery, Creation for Liberation and The Elbow Room (more of a conceptual space), all located in London, marked the independent initiatives that black artists had to create for themselves. They successfully galvanised existing talent and provided spaces for exhibitions that were otherwise non-existent. Concurrently, publicly funded museums and galleries were responding to the call from their funding bodies to make space for black artists. However, not all exhibition selections were predicated on politicised imagery or race but on the nature of the artists' practice. Today, the aforementioned London spaces no longer exist, with the exception of the Commonwealth Institute, the Africa Centre (though neither appears to have a regular contemporary exhibition programme), and the 198 Gallery, having fallen victim to the volatile fluctuations of the funding system. Instead, what remains are some sympathetic parties who realise the value of exhibiting work which reflects the cross-cultural currents within contemporary art practice.

There was discussion as to whether the exhibitions listed here would be 'black only' exhibitions. Exhibitions where black artists were the only participants were and still are necessary for placing these artists on the map of contemporary art practice. The pattern has changed to some extent and this is reflected by constructing a chronology that lists exhibitions where black artists were not the only participants. It is for the prospective researcher to discern the historical significance of this pattern. However, philosophical considerations have meant that an over-arching category of 'black only' exhibitions would necessarily locate the practice of all the

artists herein within a particular frame of reference that
is not wholly representative of those practices.
Use of the term black does not denote any specific
characteristics in the work of the artists featured in this
bibliography. Debates surrounding the definition of 'black
art' as an art form have been both intense and
inconclusive. Its validity as a way of describing the practice
of some contemporary black artists remains equivocal,
though not fully undermined.(3) Conversely, there are other
black artists who have operated beyond that framework,
preferring not to be defined by their race or categorised by
the work they produce, work which may or may not deal
explicitly with black cultural experiences. Thus, a defining
characteristic cannot be imposed on the work of all the
artists referred to in this bibliography: to impose such
homogenisation would be to refuse the particular
character of each individual's practice. Understanding
this mélange is to recognise the significance of the active
contributions these artists have made to post-war British
art as individuals, and not simply as a lumpen collective
fighting to be heard. The artists listed in this publication
reflect the diversity of British visual art practice, which
incorporates film and video, performance art and
the development of new technologies alongside more
traditional visual art forms.
Section two is a listing of individual artists.
The section includes cross-references to the previous
chronology as well as books and catalogues from both
group and solo shows – again with accompanying articles
and reviews. Each listing refers to an artist's writing and
curatorial practice, if any. Bearing in mind that this
bibliography is a selection of what is already held in the
archive, the list of artists is not exhaustive or conclusive.
A complete listing of all the artists covered in catalogues
held in the archive can still be found at Chelsea College of
Art & Design. Unfortunately, the space allowed here cannot
fully accommodate the contributions made by all those

artists within this period. Maybe, updated versions of this bibliography (published or otherwise) will expand and redefine itself to encompass artists of non-European origin practising in Britain, whose work has been overlooked not only by mainstream institutions but by their inability to fit neatly into designated categories.

The third and final section is 'General Texts'. This has been separated into ten sub-sections that identify strands which have affected and valorised the development of these artists' practices. Periodicals such as Third Text (incorporating Black Phoenix, the three editions of which are held in the library and predate Third Text), Artrage, Bazaar, Ten.8 and Black Arts in London (all now defunct except Third Text) dealt specifically with the work of black artists; however, the scope of Ten.8 and Third Text extended to a broader cultural perspective.(4)

Debates around postmodernism, feminism, cultural difference, national identity and internationalism have already produced a body of writing that analyses the cultural context in which these artists' work operates, i.e. the conditions of reception. The writers of these texts have produced seminal works that have been published in anthologies, periodicals and monographs and are brought together in the Art History and Critical Theory section. Within the area of visual art practice, there have been significant developments in film and video, photography and performance, and several important texts have emerged in recent years. Certain journals and books stand out as having recognised the importance of these media; Black Film, British Cinema, (1988), Passion: Discourses on Blackwomen's Creativity, (1990), Ten.8: Critical Decade, Black British Photography in the 80s, (1992), and Let's Get it On: The Politics of Black Performance, (1995). Within the fields of new technology and public art comparatively little has been written which embraces these art practices; however, separate sections have been included to highlight the significance of these forms of production.

Other strands running through the bibliography include the various institutional strategies which have affected the development of black artists. Within the sections on art administration and art education there are reports on the impact of funding and training. It also includes articles and published correspondence on responses to these institutional manoeuvres. Conferences and public debates, focused on issues ranging from art and immigration to black artists and white institutions, have played a pivotal role in consolidating ideas and objectives.

As only one of a kind at present, Recordings is important in tracing a documented history, but above all it is a reference book. Some of the material is difficult to obtain, such as certain unpublished conference papers, graduate and undergraduate dissertations or non-indexed periodicals, yet they can mostly be found in Chelsea's archive. The ephemera content within the archive is considerable as it was not always possible for artists to have catalogues produced; sometimes the only indication that a show had actually happened was a listing in a magazine, a press release or a private-view invitation. While this bibliography does not claim to be definitive, the wealth of material, which includes both primary and secondary sources of slides, videos, essays, catalogues, monographs, ephemera and periodicals, testifies to the breadth and calibre of black British visual art practice.

(1)   From this point onwards I will use the word 'black' – with a lower case *b* – to describe people of African, Afro-Caribbean, South East Asian and Asian descent while acknowledging it as a contentious issue and that other expressions may have been used in its place. For an introduction to the genealogy of the term see Stuart Hall, 'New Ethnicities', in Black Film, British Cinema, edited by Kobena Mercer, ICA Document 7, (London: Institute of Contemporary Arts, 1988), pp.27-30 and Kobena Mercer, 'Introduction: Black Britain and the Cultural Politics of Diaspora', in Welcome to the Jungle: New Positions in Black Cultural Studies, (London: Routledge, 1994), pp.1-32.

(2)   See Paola Barbarino, 'Focusing on Plurality and Internationalism: A New Resource in the Field of Contemporary Visual Art, The Library and Archive of the Institute of International Visual Arts', Art Libraries Journal, 20, no.3 (1995), 28.

(3)   See Rasheed Araeen & Eddie Chambers 'Black Art: A Discussion', Third Text, no.5, (Winter 1988 – 1989), 51-77; Kobena Mercer, 'Black Art and the Burden of Representation' in Welcome to the Jungle: New Positions in Black Cultural Studies, (London: Routledge, 1994), pp.223-258; Paul Gilroy, 'Cruciality and the Frog's Perspective: An Agenda of Difficulties for the Black Arts Movement', in Small Acts: Some Thoughts on the Politics of Black Cultures, (London: Serpent's Tail, 1993), pp.97-114. These are some key texts to name a few though there are other writers who have dealt with the contradictory position held by the black artist working in a British context.

(4)   The last editions of Artrage, Bazaar and Ten.8 held in the library are dated February 1995, Autumn 1992 and Spring 1992 respectively. It would appear that no subsequent copies have been published.

1978 – 1990

1978 – 1990

Composite (left to right, top to bottom):
(Magazine covers) *Bazaar: South Asian Arts Magazine,* no.1, Spring 1987
[image: 'Map of Dreams', Shobena Jeyasingh];
Black Arts in London, no.129, 1 – 31 October 1990, [image by Denzil Forrester];
Third Text, no.1, Autumn 1987.
Courtesy of Rasheed Araeen;
Artrage: Inter-Cultural Arts Magazine, no.7, Summer 1984
[image: 'How Could One Paint a Self Portrait', Rasheed Araeen]. Courtesy of Rasheed Araeen.

1978

1983

1983

1978
(Magazine cover)
Black Phoenix, no.2,
Summer 1978
[image by Rasheed
Araeen]. Courtesy
of Rasheed Araeen.

1983
(Catalogue cover)
Five Black Women,
1983. Courtesy of
Lubaina Himid.

1983
(Catalogue cover)
*The Pan-Afrikan
Connection*, 1983.
Courtesy of
Eddie Chambers.

1984

1985

1986

1984
(Poster)
*Past Imperfect, Future
Tense:* An Exhibition
of Work by Keith Piper,
1984. Courtesy of
Keith Piper.

1985
(Catalogue cover)
The Thin Black Line,
1985.

1986
(Invitation)
Unrecorded Truths,
1986. Courtesy of
Lubaina Himid.

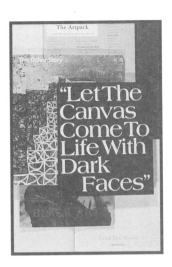

1986 – 1990
Composite (top to bottom):
(Catalogue covers) *The Artpack,* 1988.
Courtesy of Eddie Chambers;
The Other Story, 1989
[image: 'The Wall', Anwar Jalal Shemza].
Courtesy of Mary Shemza;
"Let the Canvas Come to Life with Dark Faces", 1990. Courtesy of Eddie Chambers;
The Essential Black Art, 1988
[image: 'Variation on Discord and Divisions', a performance by Mona Hatoum; photograph by Corry Wyngaarden].
Courtesy of Mona Hatoum;
From Two Worlds, 1986.
Courtesy of Whitechapel Art Gallery.

1987

1987
(Magazine cover)
Third Text, no.1,
Autumn 1987.
Courtesy of
Rasheed Araeen.

1988
(Catalogue cover)
*The Essential Black
Art,* 1988 [image:
'Variation on Discord
and Divisions',
a performance
by Mona Hatoum;
photograph by
Corry Wyngaarden].
Courtesy of
Mona Hatoum.

1987
(Catalogue cover)
*Creation for Liberation
Open Exhibition,* 1987
[image: 'Sun Hyroglyph',
Aubrey Williams].
Courtesy of Eve Williams.

1989
(Catalogue cover)
*Fabled Territories:
New Asian
Photography
in Britain,* 1989
[image: 'Water'
Juanito Wadhani].

1990
(Book cover)
*Passion: Discourses
on Blackwomen's
Creativity,* 1990
[image: 'Snakes and
Ladders', Nina Edge].
Courtesy of Maud
Sulter and Nina Edge.

1990
(Poster)
Disputed Identities,
1990 [images: detail
from: 'Infestation of
the Aorta – Shrine to
a Distant Relative',
Sutapa Biswas;
'Measures of Distance',
Mona Hatoum;
'Duel', Dianne Tani].

1992
(Magazine cover)
*Ten.8, Critical
Decade: Black
British Photography
in the 80s,*
2, no.3, Spring 1992
[image by Franklyn
Rodgers]. Courtesy
of David Bailey.

1993
Postcard, [artist's book consisting of 144
colour postcards forming one composite
image], Virginia Nimarkoh, 1993.
Courtesy of Virginia Nimarkoh.

1993

Contents of *The Phone Box: Art in Telephone Boxes,* [a book with original artists works; curated by Virginia Nimarkoh], 1993.
Courtesy of Virginia Nimarkoh.

Chronology

1971
Caribbean Artists in England.
Commonwealth Art Gallery, London, with Althea Bastien, Winston Branch, Owen R Coombs, Karl Craig, Daphne Dennison, Art Derry, Errol Lloyd, Donald Locke, George Lynch, Althea Mcnish, Ronald Moody, Keith Simon, Vernon Tong, Ricardo Wilkins, Aubrey Williams, and Llewellyn Xavier, (18pp, illus.).

1973
Eight Commonwealth Artists.
The Laing Annexe, Newcastle-Upon-Tyne, with Aubrey Williams, and Emmanuel Jegede, (18pp, illus.).

1978
Afro-Caribbean Art.
Warehouse Gallery, London, with Adiose Wallace, Shaigi Rahim, Lloyd Nelson, Orville Smith, Reynolds Duncan, Donald Locke, and Jeffrey Trotman ...et al.
_ Emmanuel Cooper, 'Afro-Caribbean Art', *Art & Artists,* (July 1978), 50.
_ Rasheed Araeen, 'Afro-Caribbean Art', *Black Phoenix,* no. 2, (1978), 30-31.

1982
The Pan-Afrikan Connection: An Exhibition of Work by Young Black Artists-Good Ideals.
The 35 King Street Gallery, Bristol, [toured], with Claudette Johnson, Keith Piper, Donald Rodney, and Eddie A.Chambers, (1 folded leaf).

1983
5 Black Women.
Africa Centre Gallery, London, with Sonia Boyce, Lubaina Himid, Claudette Johnson, Houria Niati, and Veronica Ryan, (7pp).
_ Charles Moremi, 'Beyond labels' [Five Black Women Artists], in Rozsika Parker & Griselda Pollock, *Framing Feminism: Art and the Women's Movement 1970 – 1985,* pp.258, (reprinted from *City Limits,* September 1983).
_ Sarah Kent, 'Africa Centre', *Time Out,* (6 – 12 October 1983), 88.

Black Woman Time Now.
Battersea Arts Centre, London, with Jean Campbell, Andrea Telman, Ingrid Pollard, Margaret Cooper, Mumtaz Karimjee, Elizabeth Eugene, Leslee Wills, Cherry Lawrence, Lubaina Himid, Brenda Agard, Houria Niati, Veronica Ryan, Claudette Johnson, Sonia Boyce, and Chila Burman, (press release).

Creation for Liberation: Open Exhibition of Contemporary Black Art in Britain.
St. Matthews Meeting Place, London, with Thomas [Tam] Joseph, Barry Simpson, Leslee Wills, Denzil Forrester, Johnny Ohene, Susan McFarlane, Errol Lloyd, Mueme Jiyane, and Shaheen Merali, (poster).

Heart in Exile.
An Exhibition of Drawings, Painting, Sculpture and Photography by British-based Black Artists, Black Art Gallery, London, with Eddie Chambers, Barry Simpson, Shakka Dedi, Joseph Olubo, Terence Dyer, Olive Denoes, Keith Piper, Anum Iyapo, Dee Casco, George Kelly, Wayne Tenyue,

Cherry Lawrence, Ossie Murray, Tyrone Bravo, Carl Gabriel, Vanley Burke, Pogus Ceasar, Pitika Ntuli, Funansi Gentiles, Marlene Smith, Headley Grafton, and Adrian Compton, (poster & pamphlet).

The Pan-Afrikan Connection: An Exhibition of Work by Young Black Artists.
Herbert Art Gallery and Museum, Coventry, with Claudette Johnson, Keith Piper, Donald Rodney, Eddie Chambers, Wenda Leslie, and Janet Vernon, (8pp, illus.).
_ Lubaina Himid, 'Pan Afrikan Connection' [correspondence], *Art Monthly,* (May 1983), 22-23.
_ Kevin Young, 'Art Show Row is Storm in a Tea Cup, Says Top Critic', *Art Monthly,* no.65, (April 1983), 19, (reprinted from *The Coventry Evening Telegraph,* 22 February 1983).

1984
(Second) Creation for Liberation Open Exhibition.
The Brixton Art Gallery, London, (poster).

An Exhibition of Radical Black Art by the BLK Art Group.
Battersea Arts Centre, London, with Eddie Chambers, Keith Piper, Donald Rodney, and Marlene Smith, (press release).

Into The Open: New Painting, Prints and Sculpture by Contemporary Black Artists.
Mappin Art Gallery, Sheffield, with Clement Bedeau, Slybert Bolton, Sonia Boyce, Pogus Ceasar, Eddie Chambers, Shakka Dedi, Uzo Egonu, Lubaina Himid, Gavin Jantjes, Claudette Johnson, Tom [Tam] Joseph, Juginder Lamba, Bill Ming, Tony Moo-Young, Ossie Murray, Houria Niati, Benjamin Nhlanhla, Pitika P. Ntuli, Keith Piper, Richie Riley, Veronica Ryan, Jorge Santos; Film section with Isaac Julien, Imruh Caesar, Milton Bryan, and Henry Martin, (12pp, illus.)
_ Linda Syed, 'Into the Open: New Paintings, Prints and Sculpture by Contemporary Black Artists', *Art Attack,* 3, (August – September 1984), (2-3).

The Selectors' Show.
Camerawork, London, with Mitra Tabrizian and Brenda Agard.
_ Gloria Chalmers, 'The Selectors' Show', *Ten.8,* no.16, 88-89.

1985
Black Skin/Blue Coat.
Bluecoat Gallery, Liverpool, with Sonia Boyce, Eddie Chambers, Tom Joseph, and Keith Piper, (5pp, illus.).
_ 'Black Skin/Blue Coat-Black Art Exhibition In Liverpool' (Extract from the catalogue), *Art Attack,* 5/6, (December 1984 – April 1985), 10-11.

Combinations: Lubaina Himid and Jaginder Lamba.
Cotton Gallery, Midlands Art Centre, Birmingham, (1 folded leaf).

Creation for Liberation The Third Open Exhibition: Contemporary Art by Black Artists.
GLC Brixton Recreation Centre, London, with Clement Bedeau, Chila Burman, Pogus Ceasar, Margaret Cooper, Eddie Chambers, Stella Dadzie, Atvarjeet Dhanjal, Horace Opio Donovan, Tapfuma Moses Gutsa, Amarjeet Gujral, Lubaina Himid, Anthony Jadunath, George Kelly, Errol Lloyd, Kenneth McCalla, Pitika Ntuli, Mowbray Odonkor, Eugene Palmer, Maud Sulter, Aubrey Williams, Shakka Dedi, and Amanda Holiday, (16pp).

From Generation to Generation (The Installation).
OBAALA Arts Cooperative, The Cotton Gallery, Midlands Art Centre, Birmingham [toured], with David A. Bailey, Sonia Boyce, Shakka Dedi, George Kelly, Kenneth McCalla and Keith Piper, (16pp, illus.).
_ Dave Lee, 'From Generation to Generation' [GLC Brixton Recreation Centre, London; exhibition], *Arts Review,* (14 March 1986), 133.

Eastern Views.
Museums and Art Galleries, Leicester, with Said Adrus, Saleem Ayub, Surinder Singh Juttla, Anu Patel, and Gurminder Sikand, (11pp, text by Julia Nicholson).

GLC Anti-Racist Mural Project.
GLC Race Equality Unit, London, with Tam Joseph, and Gavin Jantjes: Brixton; Dushka Ahmad, and Shanti Panchal: Tower Hamlets; Chila Kumari Burman: Southall; Lubaina Himid, and Simone Alexander: Notting Hill, (10pp, illus.).
_ Graham de Schmidt, *Signs of Resistance,* (London: GLC Race Equality Unit, 1985), (GLC Anti-Racist Mural project: video).
_ GLC Anti-Racist Murals, *Artrage,* no.9/10, (Autumn 1985), 44.
_ Anwar Tambe, 'Race Mural is Waste of Cash', *Southall Gazette,* (14 June 1985).

Hounslow Asian Visual Artists Collective (HAVAC).
The Hounslow Civic Centre, Hounslow, with Ferha Farooqui, Chila Kumari Burman, Satjit Kaur Heer, Amarjeet Kaur Guraj, Shakila Maan, Allan de Souza, and Amarjit Phull.
_ Bahauddeen Latif, 'Hounslow Asian Visual Artists Collective', *Artrage,* no.9/10, (Autumn 1985), 45.

Mirror Reflecting Darkly.
Brixton Art Gallery, London, with Brenda Agard, Zarina Bhimji, Chila Burman, Jennifer Comrie, Novette Cummings, Valentina Emenyeonj, Carole Enahoro, Elisabeth Jackson, Lalitha Jawah Irilal, Rita Keegan, Christine Luboga, Sue Macfarlane, Olusola Oyeleye, Betty Vaughan Richards, Enoyte Wanagho, and Paula Williams, (17pp, illus.).
_ *Women's Work: Two Years in the Life of a Women's Artist Group (1983 – 1985),* (London: Brixton Art Gallery, 1986), 47-52.

New Horizons: An Exhibition of Arts.
GLC Royal Festival Hall, South Bank Centre, London, with Sokari Douglas Camp, Margaret Cooper, Vijaya Patel, Brian Tai-Shen Wang, Louie Ramirez, Jonathan Fraser, Moses Tapfuma Gutsa, Tom Lal, Derek Washington Rose, Emmanuel Taiwo Jegede, Horace Opio Donovan, Lubaina Himid, Waheed Pall, Veronica Ryan, George Fowakan Kelly, and Anthony Jadunath, (61pp, illus.).
_ Nigel Pollitt, 'New Horizons', *City Limits,* (25 – 31 January 1985), 58.

Roadworks.
Brixton Art Gallery, London, with Rasheed Araeen, and Mona Hatoum.
_ Margaret Garlake, '*Roadworks* at the Brixton Art Gallery', *Art Monthly,* no.88, (July – August 1985), 17.

The Thin Black Line.
[Selected by Lubaina Himid], Institute of Contemporary Arts, London, with Brenda Agard, Chila Burman, Claudette Johnson, Ingrid Pollard, Jennifer Comrie, Lubaina Himid, Marlene Smith, Maud Sulter, Sonia Boyce, Sutapa Biswas, and Veronica Ryan, (9pp, illus.).
_ Jacob Ross, 'Talking a Thin Black Line: a Report of the ICA Seminar on its Exhibition of

Black Women Artists', *Black Arts in London,* no.48, (1 – 15 February 1986), 5-6.
– Lubaina Himid, 'From the Thin Black Line', *Artrage,* no.11, 18-19.
– Lubaina Himid, 'Letter on Exhibiting at the ICA', *Artrage,* no.12, Spring 1986, 2.
– Lubaina Himid, *The Thin Black Line,* (Hebden Bridge: Urban Fox Press, 1989), (reprint).
– Waldemar Januszczak, 'Anger at Hand', *The Guardian,* (26 November, 1985).
– Sarah Kent, 'A Thin Black Line', *Time Out,* (28 November – 4 December 1985), 33.
– Marlene Smith, 'Thin Black Line', *Women's Review,* no.4, (February 1986), 22-23.

Three Asian Artists.
Commonwealth Institute, London, with Said Adrus, Sardul Gill, and Gurminder Kaur Sikand.
– C.Jah, 'Three Asian Artists', *Art Attack,* 8, (September 1985), 14-15.

1986
Aurat Shakti: A Photographic Reflection of our Lives.
Cockpit Gallery, London [GLC presentation], with Mumtaz Karimjee, Manjula Mukherjee,
Vibha Osbon, and Amina Patel, (poster).
– Mumtaz Karimjee, and Amina Patel, 'Aurat Shakti Revisited', *Ten.8: Critical Decade:
Black British Photography in the 80s,* 2, no.3, (Spring 1992), 62-63.
– Amina Patel, 'The Settler Makes Her/History', *Polareyes,* no.1, (1987), 21.

Black Edge: Afro-Caribbean Photography in Britain.
Mappin Art Gallery, Sheffield, with David A. Bailey, Vanley Burke, Newton Brown, Armet Francis,
Madahi, and Horace Ové, (press release).

Black Women in View.
Battersea Arts Centre, London, with Carole Enahoro, Rita Keegan, Lorraine Luke, Ogu Nnachi,
Susie Nottingham, Louise Owen, Elaine Somerville, and Paula Williams, (16pp, illus.).
– 'Black Women in View: An Exhibition of Installation, Construction, Tape Slide
and Mixed Media', *Women Artists Slide Library Journal,* no.15, (February 1987), 12.
– Monique Nogozi Nri, 'Black Women in View', *Black Arts in London,* no.68,
(26 – 31 January 1987), 6-7.

Brushes With the West.
Wapping Sports Centre, London, with Achar Kumar Burman, Jennifer Comrie, Allan de Souza,
and Shafique Uddin, (7pp).

Caribbean Expressions in Britain.
[Selected by Aubrey Williams, Pogus Caesar, and Bill Ming], Leicestershire Museum and
Art Galleries, Leicester, with Simone Alexander, Frank Bowling, Sonia Boyce, Pogus Caesar,
Denzil Forrester, Anthony Jadunath, Errol Lloyd, John Lyons, Bill Ming, Ronald Moody,
Colin Nichols, Eugene Palmer, Veronica Ryan, Gregory White, and Aubrey Williams,
(22pp, illus., text by Errol Lloyd).
– Elean Hooper-Greenhill, 'Caribbean Expressions in Britain', *Arts Review,*
(26 September 1986), 513.
– Errol Lloyd, 'Introduction: An Historical Perspective' *Artrage,* no.15, (Winter 1987), 13-16,
(reprinted from the catalogue: *Caribbean Expressions in Britain*).

Conceptual Clothing.
Ikon Gallery, Birmingham, with Rasheed Araeen, Sokari Douglas Camp and Mona Hatoum,
(44pp, illus. texts by Ted Polhemus and Monica Bohm-Duchen).
– Tessa Sidey, 'Conceptual Clothing', *Arts Review,* 39, (27 February 1987), 127-128.

Darshan: An Exhibition by Ten Asian Photographers.
Camerawork, London, with Zarina Bhimji, Prodeepta Das, Ashvin Gatha, Sunil Gupta, Sunil Janah, Mumtaz Karimjee, Abida Kahn, Samina Khanour, Sarita Sharma, and Padma Shreshtha, (24pp, illus., text by Dilip Hiro).

Double Vision: An Exhibition of Contemporary Afro-Caribbean Art.
Cartwright Hall, Bradford, with Tam Joseph, Franklyn Beckford, Amanda Hawthorne, Keith Piper, Debbie Hursfield, Johney Ohene, Gregory White, Margaret Cooper, Uzo Egonu, Lee Hudson Simba, and Madge Spencer, (1 folded leaf, illus.).

From Two Worlds.
Whitechapel Art Gallery, London [toured] with, Rasheed Araeen, Saleem Arif, Franklyn Beckford, Zadok Ben-David, Zarina Bhimji, Black Audio Film Collective, Sonia Boyce, Sokari Douglas Camp, Denzil Forrester, Lubaina Himid, Gavin Jantjes, Tam Joseph, Houria Niati, Keith Piper, Veronica Ryan and Shafique Uddin, (48pp, illus., text by Adoela Solanke).
    _ Eddie Chambers, 'A Bizarre Form of Anthropology', *The Race Today Review,* (March 1987), 28-29.
    _ Dennis Duerden, 'Rage of Protest', *West Africa Magazine,* (25 August 1986), 1778-1779.
    _ William Feaver, 'A Ring on the Ethnic Doorbell', *The Observer,* (31 August 1986).
    _ 'From Two Worlds', *Black Arts in London,* no.60, (16 July – 31 August 1986), 3-5.
    _ 'From Two Worlds' [preview], *Artrage,* no.13, (Summer 1986), 41 (illustrations).
    _ Waldemar Januszczak, 'There is a World Elsewhere', *The Guardian,* (16 August 1986).
    _ Deanna Petherbridge, 'Bold Conflict of Images "From Two Worlds"', *The Financial Times,* (7 August 1986), 21.
    _ John Roberts, 'From Two Worlds' [Fruitmarket Gallery, Edinburgh], *Artscribe,* no.62, (March – April 1987).

Jagrati.
Greenwich Citizens Gallery, London, with Dushka Ahmed, Symrath Patti, Zarina Bhimji, Sutapa Biswas, Chila Kumari Burman, Nina Edge, Bhajan Hunjan, Naomi Imy, Mumtaz Karimjee, Shamina Khanour, Sukhwinder Saund, Ranjan Shadra, and Shanti Thomas.
    _ 'Jagrati: Exhibition by 13 Asian Women Artists', *Artrage,* no.15, (Winter 1986), 24-25 (illustrations only).

Reflections of the Black Experience.
GLC Racial Equality Unit and the Brixton Art Gallery, London [presented as part of the Black Experience Arts Programme], with Marc Booth, Vanley Burke, Armet Francis, Sunil Gupta, Mumtaz Karimjee, David Lewis, Zak Ove, Ingrid Pollard, Suzanne Roden, and Madahi Sharak, (28pp, illus., text by Eddie George)
    _ David A.Bailey, 'Reflections of the Black Experience', *Creative Camera,* (6 June 1986), 8.

Tangled Roots.
Brixton Art Gallery, London, with Carol Agana, Margaret Agana, Barbara Bennet, Rita Charles, Sehnaz Hanslot, Joy Kahumba, Rita Keegan, Lorna Leslie, Valerie Mason-John, Veronica Mackenzie, Glynes Nelson, Louise Owen, Alka Prabhakar, Folake Shoga, Dorothea Smart, Elaine Somerville, Jennifer Tyson, Enyote Wanogho, and Paula Williams, (26pp, illus.).
    _ 'Tangled Roots: Second Annual Exhibition of Black Women Artists', *Women Artists Slide Library Journal,* (October 1986), 7-8.

The Colours of Black: A Black Arts Showcase.
GLC Confernce Hall, London, with Rasheed Araeen, David Bailey, Chila Burman, Uzo Egonu, Armet Francis, Gavin Jantjes, Emmanuel Taiwo Jegede, George Kelly, Shaheen Merali,

Fitzroy Sang, and Aubrey Williams, (21pp, leaflet and poster).
_ '[The] Colour Black: a Varied Spectrum', *Black Arts in London,* no.49,
(20 February – 3 March 1986), 6.

Third World Within: Cross-Section of Work by Afro-Asian Artists in Britain.
Brixton Art Gallery, London, with Rasheed Araeen, David Bailey, Houria Niati and Mona Hatoum,
(press release).
_ Margaret Garlake, 'Third World Within', *Art Monthly,* no.96, (May 1986), 13-14.

Twelve Days at the Roundhouse.
The Roundhouse, London, with Chila Kumari Burman, Lubaina Himid, Tom [Tam] Joseph,
and Shanti Panchal, (leaflet and posters).

Unrecorded Truths.
The Elbow Room, London, with Brenda Agard, Simone Alexander, David Bailey,
Sutapa Biswas, Sonia Boyce, Allan de Souza, Keith Piper, Donald Rodney, and Marlene Smith,
(10pp, illustrated artists pages)
_ 'Unrecorded Truths at the Elbow Room', *Black Arts in London,* no.54, (2 – 3 May 1986), 4-5.
_ Nigel Pollitt, 'Unrecorded Truths', *City Limits,* (1 – 8 May 1986).

1987
Creation For Liberation 4th Open Exhibition: Art by Black Artists.
Brixton Village, London, with Achar Kumar Burman, Margaret Cooper, Amanda Holiday, Zil Hoque,
and Fitzroy Sang, (16pp, illus. text by Eddie Chambers).
_ Mark Currah, 'Brixton Village: Creation for Liberation Open', *City Limits,*
(29 October – 5 November 1987), 71.
_ 'Open Exhibition of Contemporary Art by Black Artists Is Back', *Black Arts in London,* no.83,
(16 – 30 September 1987), 14.

Critical Realism: Britain in 1980s Through the Work of 28 Artists.
Nottingham Castle Museum, Nottingham [toured] with Sonia Boyce, Sutapa Biswas,
Shanti Thomas, and Tam Joseph, (48pp, illus., texts by Brandon Taylor and Juliet Steyn)
_ David Lee, 'Critical Realism', *Arts Review,* (25 September 1987), 643.

Depicting History: For Today.
Mappin Art Gallery, Sheffield, [toured], with Lubaina Himid, Keith Piper, and Donald Rodney,
(33pp, illus.).

Dislocations.
[Selected by Veronica Ryan] Kettle's Yard, Cambridge with, Mona Hatoum, Simone Alexander,
Zarina Bhimji and Veronica Ryan (1 folded leaf, illlus.).
_ Michael Archer, 'Dislocations', *Art Monthly,* no.114, (March 1988), 20-21.

D-Max: A Photographic Exhibition.
Ikon Gallery, Birmingham [toured], with David A. Bailey, Marc Boothe, Gilbert John,
David Lewis, Ingrid Pollard, Zak Ové, and Suzanne Roden, (28pp, illus., texts by Paul Gilroy
and Eddie Chambers).
_ Paul Gilroy, 'D-Max' [reprinted from the exhibition catalogue], in *Small Acts:
Thoughts on the Politics of Black Cultures,* (London: Serpent's Tail, 1993), pp.115-119.
_ David A. Bailey, 'D-Max' [Ikon Gallery, Birmingham; the Photographers' Gallery,
London: exhibition], *Ten.8,* no.27, 36-41.

_ 'D-Max: a Photographic Exhibition', *Black Arts in London,* no.82, (1 – 31 August 1987).
_ David Lee, 'Photography', *Arts Review,* (31 July 1987), 519.

The Devil's Feast.
Chelsea School of Art, London, with Allan de Souza, Chila Burman, Donald Rodney,
Jennifer Comrie, Keith Piper, and Zarina Bhimji, (1 folded leaf and video).
_ Eddie Chambers, 'Problematic space: "The Devils Feast"', *Race Today,* (June 1987), 27.

The Image Employed: The Use of Narrative in Black Art.
[Selected by Keith Piper and Marlene Smith], Cornerhouse, Manchester, with Simone Alexander,
Zarina Bhimji, Sutapa Biswas, Sonia Boyce, Chila Kumari Burman, Eddie Chambers,
Jennifer Comrie, Amanda Holiday, Claudette Johnson, Tam Joseph, Mathison/George,
Mowbray Odonkor, Keith Piper, Donald Rodney, Marlene Smith, and Allan de Souza,
(23pp, illus., texts by Keith Piper and Marlene Smith).

New Robes for MaShulan.
Rochdale Art Gallery, Rochdale, Lubaina Himid with Maud Sulter,
(36pp, illus., texts by Olusa Oyeleye and the artists).

OBAALA's Marcus Garvey Centenary Show.
Black Art Gallery, London with, Steve Monerville, Fowokan (George Kelly), Linda King, Keith Piper,
Horace Opio Donovan, Olive Desnoes, Kenneth McCalla, Shakka Dedi, and Eddie Chambers,
(23pp, illus.).

Polareyes: Black Women Photographers.
Camden Arts Centre, London, with Brenda Agard, Margaret Andrews, Zarina Bhimji,
Similola Coker, Joy Gregory, Rhona Harritte, Joy Kahumbu, Mumtaz Karimjee, Linda King,
Jenny Mckenzie, Tracey Moffat, Amina Patel, Ingrid Pollard, Samena Rana, Molly Shinhat,
Maxine Walker, Sharon Wallace, Geraldine Walsh, Gloria Walsh, and Halina Zajac, (press release).
_ *Polareyes: A Journal by and about Black Women Working in Photography,* no.1, (1987)
(One-off journal produced on the occasion of the exhibition at Camden Arts Centre.).

Sight Seers: Visions of Afrika and the Diaspora.
Black Art Gallery, London, with Afia Yekwai, Elizabeth Hughes, Ifeoma Onyefulu, Jheni Arboine,
and June Reid, (1 folded leaf).

State Of The Art: Ideas And Images in The 1980s.
Institute of Contemporary Arts, London [London: Chatto & Windus], with Sonia Boyce,
Sutapa Biswas, Lubaina Himid, and Donald Rodney, (256pp, illus., text by Sandy Nairne
and video of episode 6: Identity, London: Channel 4, 1987).
_ Guy Brett, 'State of the Art: Three Views – Cultural Identity', *Studio International,* 200,
no.1016, (1987), 59-60.
_ 'State of the Art: Ideas and Images in the 1980s', *Arts Review,*
(27 February 1987), 116-117.

Testimony: Three Black Women Photographers.
Camerawork, London, with Brenda Agard, Ingrid Pollard, and Maud Sulter.
_ Lorraine Griffiths, 'Testimony: Three Blackwomen Photographers', *Women Artists Slide
Library Journal,* (April – May 1987), 15.
_ Jenny McKenzie, 'Testimony', *Ten.8.,* no.25, (1987), 66.
_ Maxine Walker, 'Testimony: Three Black Women Photographers', *Creative Camera,* no.4, 34.
_ Ancil Lawrence, 'Testimony: an Exhibition', *Dragon's Teeth*, no.26. (Spring 1987), 19.

1988

Along the Lines of Resistance.
[Selected by Sutupa Biswas, Sarah Edge and Clare Slattery], Cooper Gallery, Barnsley,
with Simone Alexander, Sonia Boyce, Chila Kumari Burman, Nina Edge, Leslie Hakim-Dowek,
Lubaina Himid & Maud Sulter, Lesley Sanderson, Marlene Smith, and Mona Hatoum,
(48pp, illus., texts by Juliet Steyn and Pratibha Parmar).
  _ Jane Beckett, 'Resistance, Continuity, Struggle' (interview), *FAN-Feminist Art News,*
    2, no.9, 4-8.
  _ Lubaina Himid & Maud Sulter, 'Along the Lines of Resistance:
    Some Contributions from the Exhibition', *FAN-Feminist Art News,* 2, no.9, 9-13.

An Element of Fantasy (...In All this Reality).
The Black Art Gallery, London, with Bruce Attah, Debbie Norton, Diana Lowe, and J.C.Quillin,
(12pp, illus.).

Black Art: Plotting the Course.
Oldham Art Gallery, Oldham [toured], with Said Adrus, Upjohn Aghaji, Georgia Belfont,
Donald Brown, Val Brown, Nina Edge, Isaiah Ferguson, Amanda Holiday, Carol Hughes,
Wendy Jarrett, Tam Joseph, Godfrey Lee, Errol Lloyd, John Lyons, Julia Millette,
Mowbray Odonkor, Paul Ogbonno, Eugene Palmer, Tony Phillips, Ray Povey,
Jaswinder Singh Purewal, Alistair Raphael, Lesley Sanderson, Mark Sealy, Gurminder Sikand,
Shanti Thomas, and Jan Wandja, (34pp, illus., text by Eddie Chambers).
  _ Mark Currah, 'Black Art: Plotting the Course' [Camden Art Centre, London; exhibition],
    City Limits, (1 – 8 June 1989).

Contemporary Art by Afro-Caribbean Artists.
198 Gallery, London [opening exhibtion], with Tony Moo-Young, George Kelly, Chris Todd,
David Matsua, Danielle Akua, Geraldine Walsh, Paul Green, Delroy Bent, Patrick Small,
Shaheen Merali, Derek Washington Rose, and Anthony Jadunath, (10pp).

The Essential Black Art.
Chisenhale Gallery, London, with Rasheed Araeen, Zarina Bhimji, Sutapa Biswas,
Sonia Boyce, Eddie Chambers, Allan de Souza, Mona Hatoum, Gavin Jantjes, and Keith Piper,
(48pp, illus., texts by Rasheed Araeen, Gavin Jantjes and Keith Piper).
  _ 'The Essential Black Art: Chisenhale Gallery' [preview], *Black Arts in London,* no.91,
    (1 – 15 February 1988), 11.
  _ Adeola Solanke, 'Growing Pains: Essential Black Art', *Art Monthly,* no.114,
    (March 1988), 21-23.
  _ Mark Currah, 'The Essential Black Art', *City Limits*, (25 February – 3 March 1988), 73.
  _ David Lee, 'Essential Black Art', *Arts Review,* (26 February 1986), 117.

Figuring Out the Eighties.
Laing Art Gallery, Newcastle, with Saleem Arif, Denzil Forrester, (24pp, illus., text by Tony Godfrey).

Gold Blooded Warrior.
Tom Allen Centre, London, with Lubaina Himid and Maud Sulter.
  _ 'Gold Blooded Warrior: New Work by Lubaina Himid & Maud Sulter', *Black Arts in London,*
    no.97, (1 – 15 May 1988), 13.

Graven Images: Art, Religion and Politics.
Harris Museum and Art Gallery, Preston,with Rasheed Araeen, Saleem Arif, Sutapa Biswas,
Arpana Caur, and Dhruva Mistry, (1 folded leaf, illus., text by Karen Southworth).

Incantations: Reclaiming Imagination.
The Black Art Gallery, London, with Georgina Grant, Amanda Holiday, Mowbray Odonkor, (15pp, illus.).
_ 'Incantations', *Black Arts in London,* no.101, (1 – 15 July 1988), 14-15.

Influences.
South London Art Gallery, London, with Sokari Douglas Camp, Keith Piper, Lubaina Himid, Simone Alexander, Joseph Olubo, and Brenda Agard, (7pp, illus.).
_ Mark Currah, 'Influences: South London Art Gallery', *City Limits,* (22 – 29 September), 79.

Mysteries.
The Black Art Gallery, London, with Roy Blackwood, Alvin Kelly, and Opio Donovan, (15pp, illus.).

Numaish Lalit Kala: Indian Arts Festival.
Bluecoat Gallery, Liverpool, with Chila Kumari Burman, Arpana Caur, Jagjit Chuhan, Amal Ghosh, Naiza Malik, Alnoor Mitha, Alistair Raphael and Shafique Uddin, (loose leaf, illus.).
_ Murdoch Lothian, 'Indian Arts Festival Exhibition', *Arts Review,* (21 October 1988), 727.
_ 'Indian Arts', *Artists Newletter,* (November 1988), 3.

Once Upon A Time: An Exhibition of Pictures and Words by Black Women Artists.
Rochdale Art Gallery, Rochdale, with Aldith Venair, Fiona Walker, Lin Tang, and Suandi, (28pp, texts by the artists).

Revelations of Black.
Greenwich Citizen's Gallery, London, with Aldith Venair, Alnoor Mitha, John Lyons, Kevin Johnson, Lin Tang, Kanta Walker, Tara Sabharwal, and Suandi, (1 folded leaf).

Spectrum Women's Festival Open Exhbition.
South London Gallery, London, with Brenda Agard, Zarina Bhimji, Pratibha Parmar, and Suzanne Roden, (32 pp, illus., texts by Liz Heron and Pratibha Parmar).

1989
The Artist Abroad: An Exhibition of Work Influenced by International Travel.
Usher Gallery, Lincoln, with Sutapa Biswas, Tam Joseph, Shaheen Merali, Vong Phaophanit, Ray Povey, and Shanti Thomas, (32pp, illus., text by Eddie Chambers).
_ Medina Hammad, 'The Artist Abroad', *Arts Review,* 42, (9 February 1990), 67-68.

Black Art: New Directions.
Stoke on Trent City Museum & Art Gallery, with Chila Kumari Burman, Anthony Daley, Amanda Holiday, Sharon Lutchman, Amrit Row, Yinka Shonibare, Dionne Sparks, and Maud Sulter, (6pp, illus., text by Andrew Lindesay).

The Cost of the English Landscape.
Laing Art Gallery, Newcastle, with Ingrid Pollard, and David A. Bailey, (32pp, illus., texts by Alan Fair, Sue Todd and Terry Morden).
_ Karen Hope, 'The Cost of the English Landscape' (Laing Art Gallery, Newcastle-upon-Tyne), *Arts Review,* (9 March 1990), 128.

Fabled Territories: New Asian Photography in Britain.
City Art Gallery, Leeds [toured], with Nudrat Afza, Zarina Bhimji, Sutapa Biswas, Chila Kumari Burman, Mujassam C-Maan, Prodeepta Das, Poulomi Desai, Allan de Souza,

Sunil Gupta, Suresh Karadia, Mumtaz Karimjee, Shaheen Merali, Mount Pleasant Photography workshop, Prathiba Parmar, and Juanito Wadhani,
(48pp, illus., text by Sunil Gupta and an extract by Hanif Kureshi).
_ Ann Cullis, 'Home Front: Fabled Territories, New Asian Photography in Britain',
  Creative Camera, no.305, (August – September 1990), 47-48.
_ 'Fabled Territories: New Asian Photography in Britain', *Bazaar,* no.10, 12-17.
_ Ali Mehdi Zaidi, 'Fabled Territories: New Asian Photography in Britain, *Bazaar,* no.11, 20.
_ Sehnaz Hanslot and Margherita Sprio, 'Other than this: "An Economy of Signs",
  and "Fabled Territories"', *Third Text,* no.13, (Winter 1990 – 1991), 49-56.
_ Maxine Walker, 'Fabled Territories', *Women's Art Magazine,* (January – February 1991), 22-2⁣
_ Shani Mootoo and Aruna Srivastava, 'Fabled Territories' [Vancouver Art Gallery, Vancouver],
  Fuse, 15, no. 4, (Spring 1992), 36-37.

Intimate Distance.
The Photographers' Gallery, London, with Ingrid Pollard, Maxine Walker, Zarina Bhimji,
Sutapa Biswas, Mona Hatoum, (1 folded leaf, illus., text by Gilane Tawadros).
_ Emmanuel Cooper, 'Intimate Distance', *Time Out,* no.990. (9 – 16 August 1989), 41.
_ Carol Enahoro, 'Intimate Distance', *Women Artists Slide Library Journal,* no. 30, (1990), 25-26.
_ Elorine Grant, 'Intimate Distance',*Spare Rib,* no.205, (September 1989), 34.
_ 'Photographers' Gallery...Intimate Distance', *Black Arts in London,* no.116. (1 – 31 July 1989), 11.
_ Veena Stephenson, 'Intimate Distances', *Bazaar,* no.9, 19.

One Spirit: Black Artists Against Racism.
198 Gallery, London, with Gavin Jantjes, Juginder Lamba, Jenny McKenzie, Shaheen Merali,
and Symrath Patti, (9pp).
_ Preethi Manuel, 'One Spirit: Black Artists Against Racism', *Bazaar,* no.8, (1989), 17.

The Other Story: Afro-Asian Artists in Post-War Britain.
Hayward Gallery, London [toured], with Rasheed Araeen, Saleem Arif, Frank Bowling, Sonia Boyce,
Eddie Chambers, Avinash Chandra, Avtarjeet Dhanjal, Uzo Egonu, Iqbal Geoffrey, Mona Hatoum,
Lubaina Himid, Gavin Jantjes, Balraj Khanna, Donald Locke, David Medalla, Ronald Moody,
Ahmed Parvez, Ivan Peries, Keith Piper, A J Shemza, Kumiko Shimizu, F. N. Souza,
Aubrey Williams, and Li Yuan Chia, (160pp, illus., texts by Rasheed Araeen, Gavin Jantjes,
David Medalla, Balraj Khanna, Guy Brett, and Mel Gooding).
_ Michael Archer, 'The Other Story', *Artscribe,* no.80, (March – April 1990), 13-15.
_ Petrine Archer-Straw, 'The Other Story', *Art Monthly,* no.133, (February 1990), 14,16.
_ Homi Bhaba & Sutapa Biswas, 'The Wrong Story', *New Statesman & Society,*
  (15 December 1989), 40-41.
_ Joan Bakewell, 'Artists Stoke Up The Race Debate', *The Times,* (3 December 1989).
_ Nancee Oku Bright, 'Black Magic and the Other World',
  Times Higher Educational Supplement, (15 December 1989).
_ John Cunningham, 'Scaling the Walls', *The Guardian,* (28 November 1989), (preview).
_ Mark Currah, 'Visual Arts- The Other Story', *City Limits,* (14 – 21 December 1989), 88.
_ Richard Dorment, 'Vexed Questions of Colour', *Weekend Telegraph,* (9 December 1989), XIII.
_ Carole Enaharo, 'The Other Story', *Women Artists Slide Library Journal,* no.31/32, 26-27.
_ William Feaver, 'The Empire Strikes Back', *The Observer,* (3 December 1989), 44.
_ Mark Fisher, 'Black Art: the Labour Party's Line', *Modern Painters,* 2, no.4,
  (Winter 1989 – 90), 77-78.
_ Andrew Graham-Dixon, 'Pride and Prejudice', *The Independent,* (5 December 1989), 19.
_ Tim Hilton, 'Collision Culture', *The Guardian*, (20 December 1989).
_ Rita Keegan, 'Over my Dead Body,' *Spare Rib,* no.209, (February 1990), 30.

_ 'Other Story: Afro-Asian Artists in Post-war Britain', *Black Arts in London,* no.119,
(1 – 30 November 1989), 10.
_ 'Other Story', [lectures and discussions], *Black Arts in London,* no.120,
(1 December 1989 – 21 January 1990), 10.
_ 'Other Story: Afro-Asian Artists in Post-War Britain...', a personal commentary
by Michelle Reeves and Anandi Ramamurthy, (London: South Bank Centre, 1989),
(published to accompany the exhibition).
_ John Russell-Taylor, 'Right Stuff, Wrong Label', *The Times,* (1 December 1989).
_ Amanda Sebestyen, 'The Other Story', *City Limits,* (30 November – 7 December 1989), 16-17.
_ Brian Sewell, 'Black Pride and Prejudice', *Evening Standard,* (4 January 1990), 25.
_ Marlene Smith, 'Another Chapter: The Other Story Exhibition', *Blackboard Review,*
no.2, (1990), 48.
_ Adeola Solanke, 'Preview: From Another World', *Art Monthly,*
(December 1989 – January 1990), 32.
_ Lola Young, 'Where Do We Go From Here? Musings on "The Other Story"',
The Oxford Art Journal, 13, no.2, (1990), 51-54.

Passion: Blackwomens Creativity of the African Diaspora.
Rochdale Art Gallery, Rochdale, with Dionne Sparks, Ingrid Pollard, Lubaina Himid,
Michelle Parkerson, and Rita Keegan, (private view invite and poster).
_ 'Passion Profiles: Dionne Sparks and Ingrid Pollard', *FAN-Feminist Art News* , 2, no. 8, (1988),
20-21, (Illustrated preview of the exhibition held at 36, Martello Street, London Fields, E8).
_ Pat Agana, 'Out of the Strong Came Forth Sweetness' [Rochdale Art Gallery, Rochdale;
exhibition], *FAN-Feminist Art News,* 3, no.1, (Summer 1989), 27.

1990

Autoportraits.
[Curated by Autograph], Camerawork, London, with Monika Baker, Allan de Souza,
Rotimi Fani-Kayode, Joy Gregory, Sunil Gupta, Mumtaz Karimjee, and Roshini Kempadoo.
_ 'Autoportraits: Autograph', *Black Arts in London,* no.122, (1 – 31 March 1990), 10.

Ask Me No Questions – I Will Tell You No Lie.
The Black Art Gallery, London, (gallery programme).
_ 'OBAALA Open Exhibition', *Black Arts in London,* no.128, (1 – 30 September 1990), 6.

The British Art Show 1990.
McLellan Galleries, Glasgow & Hayward Gallery, London, with Black Audio Film Collective,
Sonia Boyce, Mona Hatoum, Kabir Hussain, Vong Phaophanit, Veronica Ryan, Lesley Sanderson,
and Shafique Uddin, (142pp, illus., texts by David Ward and Caroline Collier).
_ Caroline Collier, 'The British Art Show', *Women's Art Magazine,* no.36,
(September – October 1990), 9-11.

Carnival in Exile: Black Photography '90.
The Black Art Gallery, London, with Vanley Burke, Kevin Small, and Larrie Paul Tierman,
(gallery programme).

Disputed Identities.
Camerawork, San Francisco, with David A. Bailey, Sutapa Biswas, Roshini Kempadoo,
Ingrid Pollard, Vincent Stokes, Mona Hatoum, and Martina Atille.
_ *SF Camerawork Quarterly: Disputed Identities,* (Fall 1990),
(published on the occasion of the exhibition).

"Distinguishing Marks".
Bloomsbury Galleries, London University Institute of Education, London, with Sonia Boyce,
Allan de Souza, Shaheen Merali, Pitika Ntuli, and Keith Piper,
(29pp, illus., texts by Jagdish Gundara, Gilane Tawadros and Maggie Semple).

Ecstatic Antibodies: Resisting the AIDS Mythology.
Ikon Gallery, Birmingham [toured], with Allan de Souza, Rotimi Fani-Kayode and Alex Hirst,
Joy Gregory, and Sunil Gupta.
    _ *Ecstatic Antibodies: Resisting the AIDS mythology*, edited by Tessa Boffin and Sunil Gupta,
      (London: Rivers Oram Press, 1990), (165+pp. illus.).
      (published to accompany the Ikon Gallery exhibition).
    _ 'Ecstatic Antibodies: Resisting the AIDS Mythology', *Black Arts in London,* no.133,
      (1 – 28 February 1991), 8-9.
    _ Emmanuel Cooper, 'Addressing Aids: Ecstatic Antibodies at Impressions, York',
      Creative Camera, no.304, (June – July 1990), 46-47.
    _ Emmanuel Cooper, 'The Censorship Debate: A British Experience', *Creative Camera,*
      no.307, (December – January 1991), 30-32.
    _ 'Salford Censors AIDS Exhibition', *Creative Camera,* no.305, (August – September 1990), 4.

The Empire's New Clothes.
Camerawork, London, with Val Brown, and Vincent Stokes, (press release).
    _ 'Empire's New Clothes at Camerawork', *Black Arts in London,* no.131-2,
      (16 December 1990 – 31 January 1991), 4.

Heritage Image & History.
Cornerhouse, Manchester, with Lubaina Himid and Ingrid Pollard,
(40pp, illus., texts by Graham Coster, Gaby Porter and Jessica Sarage).

In Focus.
Horizon Gallery, London, with Bhajan Hunjan, Chila Kumari Burman, Shanti Thomas,
Jagjit Chuhan, Mumtaj Karimjee, Zarina Bhimji, Nudrat Afza, Pradipta Das, Mali, Shafique Uddin,
Sohail, Shareena Hill, Suresh Vedak, Amal Ghosh, Prafulla Mohanti, and Ibrahim Wagh,
(31pp, illus. with additional contributions from Said Adrus, Anil Varia, Vijay Soni, Tara Sabharwal,
Zil Hoque, Allan de Souza, Naiza Mazhar Malik, Waheed Pall, Madhumita Bose Thomas,
Alnoor Mitha, and Amal Ghosh).
    _ Prasanna Probyn, 'In Focus', *Spare Rib,* no.210, (March 1990), 42.
    _ 'In Focus: 4 Exhibitions', *Black Arts in London,* no.122. (1 – 31 March 1990), 9-11.

In Sight in View: Mozaix Black Visual Arts Poster Campaign.
Various sites nationally, with Claudette Holmes, Nigel Madhoo, Roshini Kempadoo, Alvin Kelly,
Maxine Walker, and Said Adrus.
    _ 'Artists Hit the Streets', *Black Arts in London,* no.128, (1 – 30 September 1990), 6.

Journeys Through the Continents.
Westbourne Gallery, London, with Emmanuel Jegede and Osi Audu.
    _ 'Journeys Through the Continents', *Black Arts in London,* no.123, (1 – 30 April 1990), 10.

"Let the Canvas Come to Life with Dark Faces".
Herbert Art Gallery and Museum, Coventry, with Said Adrus, Olanike Adu, Osi Audu, Lanek Bauga,
Andrew Beeput, Georgia Belfont, Marcia Bennet, Chris Bramble, Donald Brown, Chila Burman,
Renganaden Calinghen, Nilifur Chowdury, Sharon Curtis, Dedar, Geta Mekonnen Deresse,
Paul Duncan, Uzo Egonu, Shreela Ghosh, Georgina Grant, Medina Hammad, Rhona Harriette,

Desmond Haughton, Colin Henry, Carlos Holder, Bhajan Hunjan, Richard Hylton, Anthony Jadunath, Winston James, Permindaur Kaur, Rita Keegan, Indra Khanna, Manjeet Lamba, Roland Lawar, Rikki Lawerence, Godfrey Lee, John Lyons, Walid Mustafa, Colin Nichols, Ingrid Pollard, Ray Povey, Jaswinder Singh Purewal, Sarah Rahim, Sher Rajah, Fitzroy Sang, Folake Shoga, Vincent Stokes, and Allan de Souza, ...et al., (66pp, illus., text by Eddie Chambers).
   _ 'Images, "Let the Canvas come to Life with Dark Faces"' [South London Gallery, London; exhibition], *Spare Rib,* no.215, (August 1990).

Louder than Words.
   Brixton Art Gallery, London, with Rita Keegan, Dorrett McKoy, and Paula Williams, (press release and poster).
   _ 'Louder than Words', *Black Arts in London,* no.130 (1 – 30 November 1990), 5.

New North: New Art from the North of Britain.
   Tate Gallery, Liverpool, with Jagjit Chuhan, Maud Sulter, and Lesley Sanderson, (76pp, illus., text by Lewis Biggs).
   _ Murdoch Lothian, 'New North', *Arts Review,* (15 June 1990), 329.

New Works for Different Places: TSWA Four Cities Project.
   [Project organised by TSWA in association with Third Eye Centre, Glasgow; Orchard Gallery, Derry; Projects UK, Newcastle; and Plymouth Arts Centre], with Mona Hatoum, Donald Rodney and Vong Phaophanit, (174pp, illus., text by Tony Foster, Jonathan Harvey and James Lingwood).
   _ Michael Archer, 'Invisible Yearnings: the TSWA Four Cities Project', *Artscribe,* no.85, (January – February 1991), 60-63.
   _ John Furse, 'TSWA Four Cities Project', *Art Monthly,* no.140, (October 1990), 14-15.

Post-Morality.
   [Open exhibition], Cambridge Darkroom & Kettle's Yard, Cambridge, with Alistair Raphael, Sunil Gupta, and Ali Zaidi, (32pp, illus., texts by Andrew Renton and Caryn Faure Walker).
   _ Brian Human, 'The Postmodern Tart', *Creative Camera,* no.308, (February – March 1991), 44-45.

Strains of War.
   Greenwich Citizens Gallery, London, with Allan de Souza, Leslie Hakim-Dowek, Walid Mustafa and Ismail Saray, (private view card).

Treatise on the Sublime.
   With Maud Sulter and Lubaina Himid, University Art Gallery, California State University, Stanislaus, (7pp, illus., text by Jane Beckett and Deborah Cherry).

The Women in my Life.
   The Small Mansion Arts Centre, London, with Ingrid Pollard, Sutapa Biswas, Zarina Bhimji (poster).

1991

Black Markets: Images of Black People in Advertising and Packaging in Britain (1880 – 1980).
Cornerhouse, Manchester, [toured], with David A Bailey, Zarina Bhimji, Sonia Boyce,
Roshini Kempadoo, Keith Piper, and Donald Rodney, (22pp, illus., text by Anandi Ramamurthy).
- Nayaba Aghedo, 'Black Markets', *Artrage,* (Summer 1991), 28-30.
- 'Black Markets', *Black Arts in London,* no.124, (1 – 30 June 1990), 8.
- 'Black Markets: Image of Black People in Advertising', *Black Arts in London,* no.130,
  (1 – 30 November 1990).
- Eddie Chambers, 'Black Markets', *Art Monthly,* no.148, (July – August 1991), 31-33.
- Emmanuel Cooper, 'Black Markets' [Royal Festival Hall, London; exhibition], *Time Out,*
  (22 – 29 May 1991), 43.
- Richard Gagola, 'Black Markets',*Creative Camera,* (December 1990 – January 1991), 47-48.
- Delta Streete, 'Black Markets', *FAN-Feminist Art News,* 3, no.8, 31.

Four x 4: Installations by Sixteen Artists in Four Gallery Spaces.
[Curated by Eddie Chambers], Harris Museum and Art Gallery, Preston,
with Shaheen Merali, Houria Niati, Sher Rajah, Lesley Sanderson; Wolverhampton Art Gallery,
Wolverhampton with Osi Audu, Val Brown, Stephen Forde, Rita Keegan; The City Gallery,
Leicester with Medina Hammad, Richard Hylton, Tony Phillips, Folake Shoga; Arnolfini,
Bristol with Permindaur Kaur, Virginia Nimarkoh, Alistair Raphael, and Vincent Stokes,
(38pp, illus., monographic texts by various authors).
- Emma Anderson, 'Four From Four x 4', *Women's Art Magazine,* no.44,
  (January – February 1992), 12-13.

History and Identity: Seven Painters.
[Curated by Eddie Chambers], Norwich Gallery, Norfolk Institute of Art and Design,
Norwich [toured], with Said Adrus, Medina Hammad, Godfrey Lee, Mowbray Odonkor,
Eugene Palmer, Tony Phillips, and Lesley Sanderson,
(21pp, illus., text by Eddie Chambers).
- 'Arts Brief', *The Times,* (8 April 1992).
- Emmanuel Cooper, 'History and Identity' [Commonwealth Institute, London; exhibition],
  Time Out, (5 – 12 February, 1992), 36.
- Charles Hall, 'History and Identity', *Arts Review,* (March 1992), 90.

Interrogating Identity.
Grey Art Gallery & Study Center, New York University, New York, with Rasheed Araeen,
Allan de Souza, Mona Hatoum, Roshini Kempadoo, Keith Piper, Ingrid Pollard, Donald Rodney
and Yinka Shonibare, (143pp, illus., text by Sarat Maharaj).
- Lois E.Nesbitt, 'Interrogating Identity', *Artforum,* (Summer 1991), 115.
- Joshua Decter, 'Interrogating Identity', *Arts Magazine,* (Summer 1991), 91.

Jashan-E-Bahar: A Spring Festival from Pakistan.
Greenwich Citizens Gallery, London, with gallery installation and festival bus by Keith Khan
and Ali Mehdi Zaidi, (private view invite and leaflet).

Mothers.
Ikon Gallery, Birmingham, with Caroline Jariwala, and Sher Rajah,
(38pp, illus., texts by Hilary Robinson, Jo Spence and Caroline Elwes).

**Shocks To The System: Social and Political Issues in Recent British Art from the
Arts Council Collection.**
South Bank Centre, London [toured], with Rasheed Araeen, Zarina Bhimji, Sonia Boyce,

Sunil Gupta, Mona Hatoum, Gavin Jantjes, Tam Joseph, David Medalla,
Vong Phaophanit, Tony Phillips, Keith Piper, Donald Rodney, Maud Sulter, and Mitra Tabrizian,
(75pp, illus.,text by Neal Ascherson)
_ 'Shocks to the System', *Black Arts In London,* no.135, (1 – 30 April 1991), 7-8.

A Table for Four.
Bluecoat Gallery, Liverpool, with Nina Edge, Bhajan Hunjan, Tehmina Shah, Veena Stephenson,
(5pp, illus.)

1992

BBC Billboard Project.
Various sites around the UK, with Ingrid Pollard, and Permindar Kaur, (1 folded leaf).

Columbus Drowning.
[Curated by Maud Sulter], Rochdale Art Gallery, Rochdale, with Lubaina Himid,
Magdelene Odundo and Veronica Ryan, (6pp, illus., text by Maud Sulter).

Confrontations.
Walsall Museum & Art Gallery, Walsall, with Chila Kumari Burman, Roshini Kempadoo,
Shaheen Merali, Lesley Sanderson, (20pp, illus.).
_ Jacques Rangasamy, 'Confrontations', *Third Text,* no.22, (Spring 1993), 99-110.

Crossing Black Waters.
City Gallery, Leicester [toured], with Said Adrus, Allan de Souza, Nina Edge, Bhajan Hunjan,
Manjeet Lamba, Shaheen Merali, and Samena Rana, (87pp, illus., texts by Allan de Souza,
Suneet Chopra and Amrit Wilson).
_ Gurminder Sikand, 'Crossing Black Waters', *Bazaar,* no.21, (Summer 1992), 20-21.

Critical Decade.
The CAVE, Birmingham.
_ Ann Cullis, 'Anthology: Critical Decade, Black British Photography in the 80s',
Creative Camera, no.318, (October – November 1992), 43-44.

The Circular Dance.
Arnolfini, Bristol [toured], with Sutapa Biswas, Chila Kumari Burman, Jagjit Chuhan, Nina Edge,
Gurminder Sikand and Shanti Thomas, (37pp, illus., text by Nima Poovaya-Smith).

The Dub Factor.
[Curated by Eddie Chambers], with Slybert Bolton, Anthony Daley, and David Somerville,
(36pp, illus., texts by Sue Hubbard, Clare Stracey, Chris Wright and postscript by Frank Bowling,
published to accompany a UK touring exhibition 1992 – 1993).

Fine Material for a Dream…?: A Reappraisal of Orientalism:
19th & 20th Century Fine Art and Popular Culture Juxtaposed with Paintings,
Video and Photography by Contemporary Artists.
Harris Museum & Art Gallery, Preston [toured], with Jananne Al-Ani, Sutapa Biswas,
Chila Kumari Burman, Nina Edge, Sunil Gupta, Mona Hatoum, Sunil Janah, Mumtaz Karimjee,
Hani Muthar, Gurminder Sikand, Elia Suleiman & Joyce Salloum, and Mitra Tabrizian,
(30pp, illus., text by Emma Anderson and Amrit Wilson).

From Where I Stand.
Brixton Art Gallery, London, with Ajamu, Henry Davis, Ian Flanders, Thabo Jaiyesimi, Paul Jones, David Emmanuel Noel, and Anthony Russell, (poster).

Icarus: A Collaboration between Juginder Lamba & Tony Phillips.
Wolverhampton Art Gallery, Wolverhampton, (private view card).

Keepin' it Together: An Exhibition by Ten Black Women.
The Pavilion, Leeds.
– 'Images', Spare Rib, (December 1992 – January 1993), 26.

New Frontiers.
Brixton Art Gallery, London, (private view invite).

Taking Flight.
The City Gallery, Leicester, with Jagjit Chuhan, Gurminder Sikand and Perminder Kaur, (press release).

Trophies of Empire: New Art Commissions in Bristol, Hull, and Liverpool.
With Keith Piper, Nina Edge, Sunil Gupta, Rita Keegan, Juginder Lamba, Shaheen Merali, Donald Rodney, Veena Stephenson, and Bandele Iyapo, (3 folded leaf pamphlets, illus).
– Trophies of Empire, (Liverpool: Bluecoat Gallery;John Moores University School of Design & Visual Arts, 1994) (72pp, illus. texts by Keith Piper, Gilane Tawadros and the artists).
– 'Images', Spare Rib, (December 1992 – January 1993), 2.
– Eddie Chambers, 'Trophies of Empire', Art Monthly, no.162, (December – January 1992), 13-15.
– Sean Cubitt, 'Going Native: Columbus, Liverpool, Identity and Memory', Third Text, no.21, (Spring 1993), 107-120.

White Noise: Artists Working With Sound.
Ikon Gallery, Birmingham, with Sonia Boyce, Richard Hylton, Rita Keegan, and Pratibha Parmar, (1 folded leaf, text by Andy Tipper).

Who Do You Take Me For?
Institute of Modern Art, Brisbane, with Sutapa Biswas, Mona Hatoum, Roshini Kempadoo, Joy Gregory, Pratibha Parmar, and Sunil Gupta, (16pp, text by Clare Williamson).

1993
African Themes
Victoria and Albert Museum, London with Faisal Abdu'Allah, and Maud Sulter.
– Leslee Wills, 'African Themes and Variations', The Weekly Journal, (11 February 1993).

Beyond Destination: Film and Video Installations by South Asian Artists.
Ikon Gallery, Birmingham, with Sutapa Biswas, Maya Chowdhry, Alnoor Dewshi, Khaled Hakim, Shaheen Merali, Sher Rajah, Alia Syed, and Tanya Syed, (36pp, illus., text by Ian Iqbal Rashid).
– Atif Ghani, 'Beyond Destination, Beyond Identity' [interview with curator, Ian Iqbal Rashid], Fuse, 18, no.1, 11-15.
– Sean Cubitt, 'Beyond Destination', Third Text, no.25, (Winter 1993 – 94), 103-104.

Black People and the British Flag.
Cornerhouse, Manchester, [London: Eddie Chambers & INIVA], with Marcia Bennet, Godfrey Brown, Dominic Hazell, Bhajan Hunjan & Said Adrus, Richard Hylton, Tam Joseph,

Anita Kaushik, Manjeet Lamba, Mowbray Odonkor, Eugene Palmer, Shilmilan Patel, Sarah Rahim, Sher Rajah, Winsome Rowe, Soulheil Sleiman, Veena Stephenson, Danijah Tafari, and Marcia Thomas, (40pp, illus., text by Lola Young).

Borderless Print.
Rochdale Art Gallery, Rochdale, with Faisal Abdu'Allah, Saleem Arif, Chris Ofili, Donald Rodney, Faisal Abdu'Allah, and Maud Sulter, (1 folded leaf, illus., text by Maud Sulter).

Captives: Keith Khan & Ali Zaidi.
Walsall Museum and Art Gallery, Walsall, 1993, (1 folded leaf, illus.).

Commonwealth Young Contemporaries.
Rhyl Library Museum & Arts Centre, Clywd with Fitzroy Sang, and Caroline Jariwala, (press release).

Disrupted Borders.
Arnolfini, Bristol, [toured], with Sutapa Biswas, Samena Rana, and Monika Baker.
_ *Disrupted Borders*, edited by Sunil Gupta, (London: Rivers Oram Press, 1993, (222pp, illus.)
_ Marina Benjamin, 'Artists on the Edge' [The Photographers' Gallery, London],
  The Independent II, (15 July 1994).
_ Liz Wells, 'Drowning in Numbers', *Creative Camera,* no.326, (February – March 1994), 46-47.
_ Althea Greenan, 'Thank You, Oprah Winfrey', *Women's Art Magazine,*
  (September – October 1993), 25.

Embers.
Harris Museum & Art Gallery, Preston, with Zarina Bhimji, Perminder Kaur, Josephine Thom, (publicity material).

Four Rooms.
Serpentine Gallery, London, with Mona Hatoum, Vong Phaophanit, and Gladstone Thompson, (30pp, illus., text by James Roberts).
_ James Roberts, 'Four Rooms', *Art & Design* [Installation Art], no.5/6, (May – June 1993) (reprinted from *Four Rooms* catalogue).

Recent British Sculpture from the Arts Council Collection.
City Museum & Art Gallery, Derby [toured], with Shirazeh Houshiary, Dhruva Mistry, and Veronica Ryan, (48pp, illus., text by Greg Hilty).

Reclaiming The Madonna: Artists as Mothers.
Usher Gallery, Lincoln, with Jagjit Chuhan, Claudette Johnson, and Folake Shoga, (48pp, illus., texts by Mary Kisler and Susan Wilson).

Transition of Riches.
Birmingham City Museum & Art Gallery, Birmingham, with Sarbjit Natt, Nilofar Akmut, Symrath Kaur Patti, Anuradha Patel, Amal Ghosh, Jagjit Chuhan, Chila Kumari Burman, and Said Adrus, (56pp, illus., texts by Cary Rajinder Sawhney and Sonali Fernando)
_ Tania Guha, 'Transition of Riches', *Third Text,* no.25, (Winter 1993 – 94), 81-86.

1994

Elements of Eve.
198 Gallery, London, with Sheila Seeparsaud-Jones, and Claudette Dunkley, (1 folded card).
_ Georgina Evans, 'Elements of Eve', *Artrage,* (February – March,1994), 22-23, 25.
_ 'Elements of Eve', *Artrage,* (April – May 1994), 11.

From Beyond the Pale.
Irish MoMA, Dublin, with Vong Phaophanit, and Maud Sulter, (112pp, illus.).

Home & Away: Seven Jamaican Artists.
October Gallery, London, with Eugene Palmer, and Danijah Tafari,
(36pp, ilus., text by Petrine Archer-Straw).

Quinta Bienal de la Habana [Fifth Havana Biennale].
Havana, Cuba, with Rasheed Araeen, Chila Kumari Burman, Sunil Gupta, Lubaina Himid,
Gavin Jantjes, Mona Hatoum, Symrath Patti, and Keith Piper, (311pp, illus.).

Seen|Unseen.
Bluecoat Gallery, Liverpool, with Uzo Egonu, Lubaina Himid, Olu Oguibe, Folake Shoga,
and Yinka Shonibare, (20pp, illus., texts by the artists).
_ Sean Cubitt, 'Seen|Unseen', *Frieze,* (November – December 1994), 60-61.

Stated Values: An Autumn Salon of Fine Paintings, Ceramics and Sculptures.
Gallery Forty-Seven, London, a 198 Gallery Presentation, with Hassan Aliyu, Eugene Palmer,
Anya Patel, Frances Richardson, George Kelly, Raksha Patel and Chris Bramble,
(private view invite).

Sculptors' Drawings presented by the Weltkunst Foundation.
Tate Gallery, London, with Shirazeh Houshiary, and Anish Kapoor, (1 folded leaf, illus.).

Us an' Dem.
The Storey Institute, Lancaster, with Faisal Abdu'Allah, Denzil Forrester, and Tam Joseph,
(14pp, boxed set with artists postcards, text by Eddie Chambers, Marlene Smith, and John Lyons).
_ 'Law and Order on New Show's Agenda', *The Lancaster Guardian,* (25 March 1994).

Visions of Darkness: A Photographic Representation of Urban Youth Culture.
198 Gallery, London, with Jennie Baptiste, and Eddie Otchere, (private view card).

Voyager: An Exploration of Asian Legacy and Contemporary Life.
Rochdale Art Gallery, Rochdale, (poster).

Walking on Sunshine.
198 Gallery, London, with Michael O'Connor, Hassan Aliyu, Johannes Phokela, Judith Henry,
Meena Jafarey, and Eugene Palmer, (private view card).

With Your Own Face On.
City Museum & Art Gallery, Plymouth, [Norwich:Wild Caret Press], with Chila Kumari Burman,
and Rita Keegan, (51pp, illus.).
_ Althea Greenan, 'Single Female Currency', *Women's Art Magazine,* no. 58,
(May – June 1994), 23-24.

1995

Boxer.
Walsall Museum & Art Gallery, Walsall, [toured] with Keith Piper, and Ingrid Pollard,
(book to be published June 1996).
_ Richard Williams, 'Blood on the Canvas', *The Guardian,* (4 August 1995), 18.
_ Piers Masterson, 'Boxer', *Art Monthly,* no.189, 34-35.

The British Art Show 4.
South Bank Centre Touring Exhibition, London, with Perminder Kaur, Steve McQueen,
and Chris Ofili, (111pp, illus., text by Richard Cork, questionnaire by Rose Finn-Kelcey).
_ James Hall, 'Butterfly Ball', *The Guardian,* (14 November 1995), 8.
_ Adrian Searle, 'British Art with Attitude', *The Independent,* (14 November 1995).
_ Robert Garnett, 'The British Art Show 4', *Art Monthly,* no.192,
(December 1995 – January 1996), 27-29.

Care and Control.
Hackney Hospital, London, with Donald Rodney, and Virginia Nimarkoh,
(London: Rear Window, 2v.).
_ Mark Sladen, 'Care and Control', *Art Monthly,* no.189, (September 1995), 13-15.

The Caribbean Connection.
Islington Arts Factory, London, with Ronald Moody, Aubrey Williams, Frank Bowling, John Lyons,
and Bill Ming, (15pp, texts by John La Rose and Errol Lloyd).

Cocido y Crudo.
Museo Nationale Centro de Arte Reina Sofia, Madrid, with Mona Hatoum, Vong Phaophanit,
and Keith Piper, (331pp, illus., texts by Jerry Saltz, Jean Fisher and Dan Cameron).

Farewell to Shadowland: A Series of Three Monographic Shows.
198 Gallery, London, with Denzil Forrester, Glasford Hunter, and Joy Gregory, (15pp, colour illus.).

Freedom.
Art Gallery & Museum, Glasgow [toured], with Oladele Bamgboye, Avtarjeet Dhanjal, Keith Piper,
and Mona Hatoum, (30pp, colour illus. text by Guy Brett).

The Impossible Science of Being: Dialogues between Anthropology and Photography.
The Photographers' Gallery, London, with Faisal Abdu'allah, Zarina Bhimji, and Dave Lewis,
(44pp, illus. texts by Christopher Davis, Christopher Pinney, Rosalind Poignant,
Michael Richardson, Michael Rowlands, Chris Wright and Lola Young).
_ Kobena Mercer, 'Art of Africa', *AN- Artists Newsletter,* (December 1995), 28-30.

Journeys West: Contemporary Paintings, Sculpture and Installation.
Chinese Arts Centre, Manchester, [toured], with Cai Yuan, Gang Chen, Ting-Fay Ho,
Xiaopeng Huang, Christopher Ku, Kwai Lau, Moses Lee, Kim Lim, Hale Man, Wenbiao Mao,
Jian Jun Xi, and Ying Sheng Yang, (38pp, colour illus., texts by Paul Huxley and Kong Changan).

Mirage: Enigma's of Race and Desire.
Institute of Contemporary Art, London, [in association with inIVA], with Isaac Julien, Sonia Boyce,
Eddie George, Trevor Mathison, Steve McQueen, Keith Khan, Susan Lewis, Ronald Fraser-Munro,
and Nina Edge, (112pp, illus., texts by Kobena Mercer, David Bailey and Catherine Ugwu).
 – Mark Sladen, 'Black on Black', *Art Monthly,* no.188, (July – August 1995), 13-15.
 – Christian Haye, 'Just an Ilusion', *Frieze,* no.24, (September – October 1995), 52-53.
 – Richard Cork, 'Bigotry Trounced in Show of Wit', *The Times,* (27 June 1995).

Moti Roti Presents: The Seed, the Root.
Brick Lane and Spitalfields, London, with Ali Zaidi, and Steve Ouditt, (guide).

Original.
[Curated by Sonia Boyce], Gasworks, London, with Marc Kearey, Virginia Nimarkoh,
Yinka Shonibare, and Johannes Phokela, (press release).

Photogenetic: Reviewing the Lens of History.
[Curated by Maude Sulter], Street Level Gallery, Glasgow, with Sonia Boyce, Chila Kumari Burman,
Lubaina Himid, Pratibha ParmAr, Ingrid Pollard, and Delta Streete, (publicity material).
 – Jane Beckett and Deborah Cherry, 'Photogenetic: Reviewing the Lens of History',
 Portfolio, no.22, 70.

Revelations.
Bonington Galleries, Nottingham, with Faisal Abdu'Allah & Clive Allen,
(7pp, illus., text by Melanie Keen).

Rites of Passage: Art for the End of the Century.
Tate Gallery, London, with Mona Hatoum, and Hamad Butt,
(152pp, illus., texts by Stuart Morgan and Frances Morris).
 – David Green and Joanna Lowry, 'Rites of Passage: Art for the End of the Century',
 Creative Camera, (October – November 1995), 38-39.
 – Adrian Searle, 'Until the End of the World', *Frieze,* no.24, (September – October 1995), 40-43.
 – Robert Garnett, 'Rites of Passage: Art for the End of the Century', *Art Monthly,* no.188,
 (July – August 1995), 28-29.
 – Lynne Cooke, 'Rites of Passage', *The Burlington Magazine,* 137, no.1110, (September 1995),
 634-635.
 – Simon Watney, 'Rites of Passage', *Artforum,* (September 1995), 86-87.*

Self-Evident.
Ikon Gallery, Birmingham, with Ingrid Pollard, Maxine Walker, and Oladele Ajiboye Bamgboye,
(55pp, illus., text by Kobena Mercer).
 – Martina Atille, 'Scared of You', *Women's Art Magazine,* no. 67,
 (November – December 1995), 20-21.
 – Okwui Enwezor, 'Occupied Territories: Power, Access and African Art', [africa95], *Frieze,*
 no.26, (January – February 1996), 37-41.
 – Kobena Mercer, 'Art of Africa', *AN-Artists Newsletter,* (December 1995), 28-30.

Phaophanit & Piper
Angel Row Gallery, Nottingham, [toured],
(26pp, illus., texts by Janice Cheddie and Clare Obussier)
 – David Green, 'Vong Phaophanit and Keith Piper', *Creative Camera,* (June – July 1995), 37.
 – Richard Hylton, 'Phaophanit and Piper', *Third Text,* no.31, (Summer 1995), 95-96.

1996

From Negative Stereotype to Positive Image.
Watershed Media Centre, Bristol [originated in 1993 by Birmingham Central Library],
with Vanley Burke, and Claudette Holmes, (1 folded leaf, illus.).

Imagined Communties.
South Bank Centre Touring Exhibition, London, with Denzil Forrester, and Yinka Shonibare,
(60pp, illus. text by Kobena Mercer).

Picturing Blackness in British Art.
Tate Gallery, London, with Sonia Boyce, Lubaina Himid, Ronald Moody, and F. N. Souza,
(1 folded leaf, text by Paul Gilroy).
 _ Tania Guha, 'Picturing Blackness in British Art', *Time Out,* (10 – 17 January 1996), 46.
 _ Michael Clarke, 'Paint it Black, Then and Now', *Times Educational Supplement,*
 (8 December 1995), 13.

Individual Artists

Abdu' Allah, Faisal
b.1969, London, England.
Group exhibitions:
1993 *Borderless Print*, see Chronology.
1994 *Us an' Dem,* see Chronology.
1995 *Make Believe,* (in collaboration with Clive Allen), Royal College of Art Galleries and other sites around London, (text by Melanie Keen).
1995 *Revelations,* see Chronology.
1995 *The Impossible Science of Being,* see Chronology.
Reviews, articles, texts, etc.:
 _ Sarah Kent, 'Developing Talents', *Time Out,* (12 – 19 January 1994), 16.
 _ Sarah Kent, 'Make Believe', *Time Out,* (22 February – 1 March 1995), 46.
 _ 'The Last Supper', *Artrage,* (February 1995), 34-35.
 _ Val Williams, 'About Face: Presences at the Photographers Gallery', *Creative Camera,* no.28, (June – July 1994), 48-49.

Adrus, Said
b.1958, Kampala, Uganda.
Group exhibitions:
1985 *Eastern Views: Works by Young Asian Artists from the Midlands,* see Chronology.
1985 *Three Asian Artists,* see Chronology.
1988 *Black Art: Plotting the Course,* see Chronology.
1988 *Paintings by Said Adrus – Ceramics by Louise Block,* Horizon Gallery, London.
1990 *In Focus,* see Chronology.
1990 *In Sight, in View,* see Chronology.
1990 *"Let the Canvas Come to Life with Dark Faces",* see Chronology.
1991 *History and Identity: Seven Painters,* see Chronology.
1992 *Black People and the British Flag,* see Chronology.
1992 *Crossing Black Waters,* see Chronology.
1993 *Transition of Riches,* see Chronology.
Reviews, articles, texts, etc.:
 'It Ain't Ethnic', *Black Arts in London,* no.128, (1 – 30 September 1990), 5.

Afza, Nudrat
b.1955, Rawalpindi, Pakistan.
Group exhibitions:
1989 *Fabled Territories,* see Chronology.
1990 *In Focus,* see Chronology.
Reviews, articles, texts, etc.:
 _ *Extending Frontiers: Black artists at Work,* (Bradford: Yorkshire Arts, 1988).
 _ Nudrat Afza, 'Photographs', *FAN-Feminist Art News,* 2, no.9, 16-17.
 _ Sara Worrall, 'Fruit and thistles: Nudrat Afza', *Bazaar,* no.11, (1990), 7-8.

Agard, Brenda
Dates Unavailable.
Group exhibitions:
1983 *Black Woman Time Now,* see Chronology.
1984 *The Selectors' Show,* see Chronology.
1985 *Mirror Reflecting Darkly,* see Chronology.

1985 *The Thin Black Line,* see Chronology.
1986 *Unrecorded Truths,* see Chronology.
1987 *Testimony: Three Black Women Photographers,* see Chronology.
1988 *Spectrum Women's Photography Festival Open Exhibition,* see Chronology.
Reviews, articles, texts, etc.:
 _ Brenda Agard, 'Photography: an Extension of…', *Polareyes,* no.1, (1987), 10-11.
 _ Maxine Walker, 'Testimony: Three Black Women Photographers', *Creative Camera,* no.4, (1987), 34.

Ahmad, Dushka
b.1960, Place of Birth Unavailable.
Group exhibitions:
1985 *GLC Anti-Racist Mural Project,* see Chronology.
1985 *Signs Of Resistance,* see Chronology.
1986 *Jagrati,* see Chronology.

Ajamu
Dates Unavailable.
Solo exhibitions:
1994 *Black Bodyscapes,* Camerawork, London, (press release).
Group exhibitions:
1992 *From Where I Stand,* see Chronology.
Reviews, articles, texts, etc.:
 _ 'Bodyscapes: Black Male Photographic Portraits', *Black Arts in London,* no.134, (1 – 31 March 1991), 6.
 _ Alex Hirst, 'Black & Beyond', *Creative Camera,* no.316, (June – July 1992), 30-34.
 _ Peter Ride, 'Black Bodyscapes', *Creative Camera,* (October – November 1994), 39.

Akmut, Nilofar
Dates Unavailable.
Group exhibitions:
1993 *Transition of Riches,* see Chronology.
1994 *An Intelligent Rebellion,* see Chronology.
Reviews, articles, texts, etc.:
 'Differences', *Black Arts in London,* no.136, (1 – 30 June 1991), 6, (198 Gallery, London).

Akomfrah, John (see also Black Audio Film Collective)
b.1957, Place of Birth Unavailable.
Group exhibitions:
1992 *Arrows of Desire: the Second Biennal of Independent Film and Video,*
    selected by Peter Wollen, (London: Institute of Contemporary Art,1992),
    [The Touch of the Tar Brush, pp.19].
Reviews, articles, texts, etc.:
 _ John Akomfrah, 'On the Borderline', *Ten.8,* 2, no.1, (Spring 1991), 50-67.
 _ 'Entretien avec John Akomfrah/An Interview with John Akomfrah', *Revue Noire,* no.1, (1991), 29-30.

Al-Ani, Jananne
b.1966, Kirkuk, Iraq.
Group exhibitions:
1992 *Fine Material for a Dream…?: A Reappraisal of Orientalism,* see Chronology.
1994 *Who's Looking at the Family,* Barbican Art Gallery, London.
1995 *Natural Settings,* Chelsea Physic Garden, London.

Alexander, Karen
Dates Unavailable.
Reviews, articles, texts, etc.:
Mica Nava, 'Karen Alexander: Video Worker', (interview), *Feminist Review,* no.18, (Winter 1984), 28-43.

Alexander, Simone
b.1964, London, England.
Group exhibitions:
1985 *GLC Anti-Racist Mural Project 1985,* see Chronology.
1986 *Caribbean Expressions in Britain,* see Chronology.
1986 *Unrecorded Truths,* see Chronology.
1987 *Dislocations,* see Chronology.
1987 *The Image Employed: the Use of Narrative in Black Art,* see Chronology.
1988 *Along the Lines of Resistance: An Exhibition of Contemporary Feminist Art,* see Chronology.
1988 *Influences,* see Chronology.
1988 *Employing the Image: Making Space for Ourselves,* directed by Amanda Holiday, London, (video).

Araeen, Rasheed
b.1935, Karachi, Pakistan.
Solo exhibitions:
1984 *Rasheed Araeen: Recent Work,* Pentonville Gallery, London.
1986 *Rasheed Araeen: White Power Black Sexuality,* Pentonville Gallery, London.
1987 *From Modernism to Postmodernism: Rasheed Araeen – a Retrospective 1959 – 1987,* Ikon Gallery, Birmingham, [toured].
1990 *Golden Verses: a Billboard Artwork by Rasheed Araeen in Collaboration with the Artangel Trust on National Display from May 1990,*1990, (leaflet).
1991 *Rasheed Araeen: What's it all about Bongo?,* Central Space, London, [Installation and continuation of *"Golden Verses"* billboard project].
1995 *Rasheed Araeen:* South London Gallery, London.
Group Exhibitions:
1985 *Roadworks,* see Chronology.
1986 *Conceptual Clothing,* see Chronology.
1986 *From Two Worlds,* see Chronology.
1986 *Third World Within,* see Chronology.
1986 *The Colours of Black,* see Chronology.
1987 *State of the Nation,* Herbert Art Gallery & Museum, Coventry.
1988 *Edge 88,* (London Performance Festival 13 – 25 September 1988), *Performance,* Special Issue, no.55, (1988).
1988 *Graven Images,* see Chronology.
1988 *The Essential Black Art,* see Chronology.

1989 *Magiciens de la Terre,* Centre Georges Pompidou, Paris.
1990 *Approaches to Realism,* Bluecoat Gallery, Liverpool.
1990 *New Necessity: First Tyne International 1990,* Gateshead.
1991 *Interrogating Identity,* see Chronology.
1991 *Recent History* [curated by Art in Ruins], Herbert Read Gallery, Kent Institute of Art & Design, Canterbuty.
1991 *Shocks to the System: Social and Political Issues in Recent British Art from the Arts Council Collection,* see Chronology.
1994 *Quinta Bienal de la Habana,* see Chronology.

Texts by Rasheed Araeen:
[n.d.] Rasheed Araeen, '"Paki Bastard": Portrait of the Artist as a Black person', *Black Phoenix,* no.2, 12-17.
1981 Rasheed Araeen, 'Showing G & G', [correspondence], *Art Monthly,* no.51, (November 1981), 28-29.
1984 Rasheed Araeen, *Making Myself Visible,* (London: Kala Press, 1984), (introduction by Guy Brett).
1984 Rasheed Araeen, 'Radical Perspectives, Indifferent Performance', *Art Monthly,* no.79, (September 1984), 26-27. (correspondence – reply to Michael Archer article, *Art Monthly,* no.78, July – August 1984).
1985 Rasheed Araeen, 'Black Representation', *Art Monthly,* (February 1985), 27, (correspondence – reply to Peter Dormer, *Art Monthly,* December 1984 – January 1985).
1986 Rasheed Araeen, *History of Black Artists in Britain,* (London: GLC Race Equality Unit, unpublished papers).
1986 Rasheed Araeen: Comments on his Works Included in the Exhibition "Two Worlds" held at the Whitechapel Art Gallery, London, September 1986, *Audio Arts,* 8, nos.2 & 3, Tape 2, Side 2.
1988 Rasheed Araeen, 'Come on, Cheer up!', *Art Monthly,* no.59, (September 1982), 29-32, (reprinted in *Storms of the Heart,* edited by Kwesi Owusu, London, 1988, pp.119-127).
1989 Rasheed Araeen, 'Our Bauhaus others' Mudhouse', *Third Text,* no.6, (Spring 1989), 3-14, (Introductory essay to a special issue of essays from *Les Cahiers du Musee National d'art Moderne,* published to coincide with the exhibition *Magiciens de la Terre,* Pompidou Centre and Parc de Villette, Paris, 1989).
1989 Rasheed Araeen, *The Other Story* [collection of 6 essays], Hayward Gallery, London.
1990 Rasheed Araeen, 'The Emergence of Black Consciousness in Contemporary Art in Britain' in *Lotte or the Transformation of the Object,* Stadtmuseum, Graz, (reprinted from *The Essential Black Art,* Chisenhale Gallery, London, 1988, pp.67-74)
1991 Rasheed Araeen, 'Modernism, History and Others: Why are Non-European Artists Invisible in Modern Discourse?', *AICARC,* nos.29 & 30, 43-47.
1992 Rasheed Araeen, 'Wer bin ich? Woher Komme ich?', *Kunstforum International,* no.118, (1992), 233-235
1992 Rasheed Araeen, 'How I Discovered My Oriental Soul in the Wilderness of the West', *Third Text,* no.18, (Spring 1992), 85-102.
1993 Rasheed Araeen, 'Gravity and [Dis] Grace', *Third Text,* no.22, (Spring 1993), 93-97.
1994 Rasheed Araeen, 'New Internationalism, or the Multiculturalism of Global Bantustans,' in *Global Visions,* (London: Kala Press; inIVA 1994), pp.3-11.
1995 Hou Hanru, 'An Interview with Rasheed Araeen', *Art and Asia Pacific,* 2, no.1, (1995), 103-107.

Reviews:
– Nayaba Aghedo, 'Rasheed Araeen's Blood & Sugar', *Artrage,* no.21, (Autumn 1988), 31-32.
– Michael Archer, 'Visual effects', *Art Monthly,* (July – August 1984), 21-22.
– Guy Brett, 'Rasheed Araeen' [Pentonville Gallery, London; exhibition], *Art Monthly,* no.94, (March 1986), 19-20.
– Guy Brett, 'Rasheed Araeen's London Billboards', *Art in America,* (March 1991), 147-148.

- Michael Corris, 'Rasheed Araeen', *Artforum,* (March 1995), 100.
- Jean Fisher, 'Rasheed Araeen', [Ikon Gallery, Birmingham; exhibition], *Artforum,* (March 1988), 155.
- Margaret Garlake, 'Rasheed Araeen' [Ikon Gallery, Birmingham; exhibition], *Art Monthly,* no.113, (February 1988), 18-19.
- Clare Harris, 'Rasheed Araeen: the Story of Subversion', *Bazaar,* no.18, (Autumn 1991), 12-13.
- John Lyons, 'A Review of Rasheed Araeen's Retrospective Exhibition "From Modernism to Postmodernism"', *Bazaar,* no.6, 23-24.
- Paul Overy, 'Rasheed Araeen', [Central Space, London; exhibition], *Art Monthly,* (April 1991), 19-21.
- Andrea Rehberg, 'Rasheed Araeen' [Ikon Gallery, Birmingham; exhibition], *Flash Art,* no.139, (March – April 1988), 121-122.
- Amanda Sebestyen, 'A Cruiser's Guide...the Outside Edge', [Showroom, London; exhibtion], *Art Line,* 4, no.4, (December 1988 – January 1989), 36.
- Gilane Tawadros, 'Rasheed Araeen', [The Showroom, London; exhibition], *Artscribe,* no.74 (March – April 1989), 74.
- Hannah Vowles and Glyn Banks, 'The Art of Difference', *Marxism Today,* (January 1989), 58-59.
- Jonathan Watkins, 'Rasheed Araeen' [The Showroom, London; exhibition], *Art International,* no.6, (Spring 1989), 54-55.

Articles:
- Rudolf Baranik, 'On AM Polemics', *Art Monthly,* no.86, (May 1985), 23-24, (correspondence – reply to Amal Chakrovarty's letter, *Art Monthly,* no.84, March 1985).
- Guy Brett, 'Both Author and Reader', *C Magazine,* no.36, (Winter 1993), 18-28.
- Guy Brett, 'Rasheed Araeen – "Making Myself Visible"', *Arts and the Islamic World,* (Winter 1984 – 1985), 77-78.
- Amal Chakrovarty, 'More on Mr. Araeen', [correspondence], *Art Monthly,* no.84, (March 1985), 21-22.
- Uzo Egonu, 'Character Assassination...' *Art Monthly,* no.86, (May 1985), 22. (correspondence – reply to Amal Chakrovarty's letter, *Art Monthly,* no.84, March 1985).
- Gavin Jantjes, 'Character Assassination...' *Art Monthly,* no.86, (May 1985), 22-23, (correspondence – reply to Amal Chakrovarty's letter, *Art Monthly,* no.86, March 1985).
- Danny Padmore, '"Making myself Visible" [by] Rasheed Araeen', *ILEA: Multi-Ethnic Education Review,* (Winter – Spring 1985), 26-28.
- Ivan Peries, 'Character assassination' *Art Monthly,* no.86, (May 1985), 22. (correspondence – reply to Amal Chakrovarty's letter, *Art Monthly,* no.84, March 1985).
- John Roberts, 'Postmodernism and the Critique of Ethnicity', in *Postmodernism, Politics and Art,* (Manchester: Manchester University Press, 1990), pp.182-194.

Arif, Saleem
b.1949, Hyderabad, India.
Solo exhibitions:
1991 *Saleem Arif: Paintings, 1986 – 1991,* Tyne and Wear Museums, Newcastle-upon-Tyne, (text by Tony Godfrey).
Group exhibitions:
1986 *From Two Worlds,* see Chronology.
1988 *Eight Contemporary British Artists,* Galerie Sapet, Valence.
1988 *Figuring Out the Eighties,* see Chronology.
1988 *Graven Images: Art, Religion and Politics,* see Chronology.
1989 *The Other Story,* see Chronology.

1991 *Surface and Symbol,* K Gallery, London, (text by David Cohen).
1993 *Borderless Print,* see Chronology.
Reviews, articles, texts, etc:
– Mary Rose Beaumont, [Anderson O'Day, London, exhibition], *Arts Review,* (18 November 1988), 816.
– Amal Ghosh, 'Shapes in Space: Saleem Arif' [Anderson O'Day, London; exhibition], *Artrage,* no.22/23, (Winter 1988), 53.
– Sue Hubbard, 'The Art of Saleem Arif', *Third Text,* no.27, (Summer 1994), 37-44.
– Helga Prosser, [Laing Art Gallery, Newcastle-upon-Tyne, England; travelling exhibition], *Arts Review,* (May 1991), 271.
– Anandi Ramamurthy, 'Saleem Arif: Drawing into Discovery' [Air Gallery, London; exhibition], *Bazaar,* no.2, (Summer 1987), 1.
– Hilary Robinson, 'Saleem Arif: Artists of a Diaspora' [interview], *Alba,* 1, no.3, (June – July 1991), 28-29.
– 'Saleem Arif: An Exhibition of Paintings 1986 – 1991', *Black Arts in London,* no.136, (1 – 30 June 1991), 6, (Laing Art Gallery, Newcastle-upon-Tyne).
– Philip Wright, 'Saleem Arif's Inferno', *Artrage,* no.2, (February 1983), 5-6.

Audu, Osikhena
b.1955, Nigeria.
Group exhibitions:
1990 *Journeys Through the Continents,* see Chronology.
1990 *"Let the Canvas Come to Life with Dark Faces",* see Chronology.
1991 *Four x 4,* see Chronology.
Reviews, articles, texts, etc.:
– Emma Burn, 'Osikhena Audu' [The Westbourne Gallery, London; exhibition], *Arts Review,* (2 November 1990), 592.
– 'Westbourne Gallery', *Black Arts in London,* no.30, (1 – 30 November 1990), 5.

Bailey, David
b.1961, England.
Solo exhibitions:
[n.d.] David Bailey, *Appropriation & Control: a Photographic Exploration of Black Images,* (London: Camerawork).
Group exhibitions:
1985 *From Generation to Generation, (The Installation),* see Chronology.
1986 *Black Edge,* see Chronology.
1986 *Unrecorded Truths,* see Chronology.
1986 *The Colours of Black,* see Chronology.
1986 *Third World Within,* see Chronology.
1987 *D-Max: A Photographic Exhibition,* see Chronology.
1990 *Disputed Identities,* see Chronology.
1991 *Black Markets,* see Chronology.
Texts by David Bailey:
1992 David A. Bailey, 'Aspects of the Liberal Dilemma' [Adrian Piper], *Frieze,* no.1, (1992), 14-16.
1986 David A. Bailey, *Synopsis of a Paper on Black Photographers and the Black Visual Arts,* (London: Greater London Council, Race Equality Unit, 1986), [unpublished papers].
1987 David A. Bailey, [Centre pages] *Block,* no.13, (1987 – 1988), 43-46.
1988 David A. Bailey, 'Black Photography: Identity and Subjectivity', in *Storms of the Heart,* edited by Kwesi Owusu, (London: Camden Press, 1988), pp.161-172.

Reviews, articles, etc:
- Paul Gilroy, 'David A. Bailey from Britain, Barbados or Both? Exploration of Black Images by David A.Bailey, 1984 – 1985', *Creative Camera,* no.2, (1990), 10-13, [Shortened version of the text that accompanied the exhibition *I'm Black, I'm Bajan and I'm British,* Tom Allen Centre, London, 1989].
- Paul Gilroy, 'On the Beach', in *Small Acts: Some Thought on the Politics of Black Cultures,* (London: Serpent's Tail, 1993), pp.146-152.
- 'I'm Black, I'm Bajan, I'm British', *Black Arts in London,* no.120, (1 December – 31 January 1990), 10, (Tom Allen Centre, London).
- Ifemu Omari, 'Positive Images of Black People: Photographs by David A. Bailey', *Ten.8,* no.16, (Review of the People's Gallery show, London, September 1984).
- Giliane Tawadros, 'Other Britains, Other Britons', *Aperture,* no.113, (Winter 1988), 40-46.

Bamgboye, Oladele Ajiboye
b.1963, Nigeria.
Group exhibitions:
1995 *Freedom,* see Chronology.
1995 *Self-Evident,* see Chronology.
Reviews, articles, texts, etc.:
- 'Artists Page: Oladele Ajiboye Bamgboye, ...Arise...', *Alba,* 1, no.4, (August – September 1991), 24-25.
- Oladele Bamgboye, 'The Hair of the Man', *Grey Suit,* no.9, (Spring 1995), (video).

Beckford, Franklyn
b.1963, London, England.
Group exhibitions:
1986 *Double Vision,* see Chronology.
1986 *From Two Worlds,* see Chronology.
Reviews, articles, texts,.etc.:
Susan Morris, 'Forms of Intuition', *Arts Review,* (5 May 1989), 356.

Bedeau, Clement Attlee
b.1950, Aruba.
Group exhibitions:
1984 *Into the Open New Painting, Prints and Sculpture by Contemporary Black Artists,* see Chronology.
1985 *3rd Creation for Liberation*, see Chronology.

Belfont, Georgia
b.1961, London, England.
Group exhibitions:
1988 *Black Art: Plotting the Course,* see Chronology.
1990 *"Let the Canvas Come to Life with Dark Faces",* see Chronology.

Bennet, Marcia
b.1968, England.
Group exhibitions
1990 *"Let the Canvas Come to Life with Dark Faces"*, see Chronology.
1993 *Black People and the British Flag*, see Chronology.

Bhimji, Zarina
b.1963, Uganda, East Africa.
Solo exhibitions:
1992 *Zarina Bhimji: I Will Always Be Here*, Ikon Gallery, Birmingham, (introduction by Mark Haworth-Booth).
1995 *Zarina Bhimji*, Kettle's Yard, Cambridge, (introduction by Marina Warner).
Group exhibitions:
1985 *f.stops*, Chelsea School of Art, London.
1985 *Mirror Reflecting Darkly*, see Chronology.
1986 *Darshan*, see Chronology.
1986 *From Two Worlds*, see Chronology.
1986 *Jagrati*, see Chronology.
1987 *The Image Employed: the Use of Narrative in Black Art*, see Chronology.
1987 *Polareyes*, see Chronology.
1987 *The Devils Feast*, see Chronology.
1987 *Dislocations*, see Chronology.
1988 *Spectrum Women's Photography Festival Open Exhibition*, see Chronology.
1989 *Fabled Territories*, see Chronology.
1989 *Intimate Distance*, see Chronology.
1990 *In Focus*, see Chronology.
1990 *Passing Glances: Works by 5 Artists Presented by Artangel in Collaboration with the British Library*, (New British Library Street Gallery, Euston Road, London, Summer 1990).
1990 *The Women in My Life*, see Chronology.
1991 *Shocks to the System: Social and Political Issues in Recent British Art from the Arts Council Collection*, see Chronology.
1993 *On Taking a Normal Situation*, Museum van Hedendaagse Kunst, Antwerpen.
1995 *The Impossible Science of Being*, see Chronology.
Texts by Zarina Bhimji:
1987 Zarina Bhimji, 'And Then I Woke Up', *Polareyes*, no.1, 8-9.
1990 Zarina Bhimji, 'Live for Sharam and Die for Izzat', in *Identity: Community, Culture, Difference*, edited by Jonathan Rutherford, (London: Lawrence & Wishart, 1990), pp.127-156.
1992 Zarina Bhimji, (Sound Recording), *Audio Arts Magazine*, 12, no.1.
Reviews, articles, etc.:
– 'Zarina Bhimji: the Culture Closet', *Creative Camera*, (April – May 1991), 36-37.
– Zarina Bhimji, 'What she herself…Was…Is…Would Like to Be', *Bazaar*, no.1, (Spring 1987), 14-15.
– 'Zarina Bhimji: She Loved to Breathe – Pure Silence', *Third Text*, no.3/4, (Spring – Summer 1988), 96-104.
– 'Zarina Bhimji, [Untitled: Five Red Petals on a Black Ground]', *Creative Camera*, no.321, (April – May 1993), 19.
– 'Zarina Bhimji: Public Art Commission', *Portfolio*, no.21, (1995), 22-23.
– Zarina Bhimji, '1822 – now', *Art History*, 18, no.2, (June 1995), 149-153.
– Tania Guha, 'L'Histoire de l'Oeil: Zarina Bhimji and Catherine Yass', *Portfolio*, no.21, (1995), 48-50.

_ Tania Guha, 'Zarina Bhimji, South London Gallery', *Time Out,* (22 – 29 March 1995), 44.
_ *Employing the Image: Making Spaces for Ourselves,* directed by Amanda Holiday, London, 1989, (video).
_ Jaki Irvine, 'Zarina Bhimji: I Will Always be Here', *Third Text,* no.22, (Spring 1993), 107-110.
_ Kellie Jones, 'In their own Image', *Artforum,* (November 1990), 132-138.
_ Mica Nava, 'The Women in my Life', *Feminist Review,* no.36, (Autumn1990), 42-45.
_ Kamaljit Sangha, 'Zarina Bhimji', *Bazaar,* no.7, 24, (Tate Gallery, Liverpool, installation).
_ GilianeTawadros, 'Other Britains, other Britons', *Aperture,* no.113, (Winter 1988), 40-46.
_ 'Tom Allen Centre', *Black Arts In London,* no.117, (1 – 30 September 1989), 10-11.
_ Marina Warner, 'A Chilling Bedside Manner', *The Independent,* (4 March 1995), (Review of Kettle's Yard, Cambridge, and South London Gallery exhibitions).

Biswas, Sutapa
b.1962, Bolpur, India.
Solo exhibitions:
1987 *Sutapa Biswas,* Horizon Galley, London.
1992 *Synapse: Sutapa Biswas,* The Photographers' Gallery, London, (texts by Gilane Tawadros and David Chandler).
Group exhibitions:
1985 *The Thin Black Line,* see Chronology.
1986 *The Issue of Painting,* Rochdale Art Gallery.
1986 *Jagrati,* see Chronology.
1986 *Unrecorded Truths,* see Chronology.
1987 *Creation for Liberation Open Exhibition,* see Chronology.
1987 *Critical Realism: Britain in the1980's through the Work of 28 Artists,* see Chronology.
1987 *State of the Art,* see Chronology.
1987 *The Image Employed: The Use of Narrative in Black Art,* see Chronology.
1988 *Along the Lines of Resistance: an Exhibition of Contemporary Feminist Art,* see Chronology.
1988 *The Essential Black Art,* see Chronology.
1988 *Graven Images,* see Chronology.
1989 *Fabled Territories,* see Chronology.
1989 *The Artist Abroad,* see Chronology.
1989 *Intimate Distance,* see Chronology.
1989 *The Other Story,* see Chronology.
1990 *Disputed Identities,* see Chronology.
1992 *Fine Material for a Dream…? A Reappraisal of Orientalism,* see Chronology.
1992 *Circular Dance,* see Chronology.
1992 *Who Do You Take Me For?,* see Chronology.
1993 *Beyond Destination,* see Chronology.
1993 *Disrupted Borders,* see Chronology.
Texts by Sutapa Biswas:
1995 Sutapa Biswas, 'Arpana Caur', in *Inside Out: Contemporary Women Artists of India,* Middlesbrough Art Gallery.
1990 'Chanting Heads: Keith Piper, Sutapa Biswas, John Carson, and Paul Gilroy', *And-Journal of Art and Art Education,* no.21, 37-43.
1990 'Section Three Portfolio – Sutapa Biswas' in *Passion,* (Hebden Bridge: Urban Fox Press, 1990), pp.202-203.
1988 'Sutapa Biswas [Interview]' in *Extending Frontiers: Black Artists at Work,* (Bradford: Yorkshire Arts).
1986 Sutapa Biswas, 'Tracing a history – What Ever Happened to Cricket?', *Ten.8,* no.22,10-15.

Reviews, articles, etc.:
- Pennina Barnett, 'Artists and Racism', [Sutapa Biswas and the racist incident at the AIM Gallery, Middlesbrough], *AN-Artists Newsletter,* (December 1987), 24-25.
- Mark Currah, 'The Issue of Painting', *City Limits,* (18 – 25 September 1986).
- Mark Currah, 'Horizon: Sutapa Biswas', *City Limits,* (2 – 9 July 1987).
- Allan de Souza, 'Graven images: art, religion and politics', *Bazaar,* no.5, (Summer 1988), 21-22, [Preston, Harris Gallery, April – May 1988].
- Yvonne Deane, 'Bhangra Girls', *FAN-Feminist Art News,* 3. no.1, (Summer 1989), 24.
- Razia Iqbal, 'Sutapa Biswas', *Bazaar,* no.6, (1988), 4-9.
- 'The Issue of Painting', *Black Arts in London,* no.62, (16 – 30 September 1986), 8.
- Griselda Pollock, 'What's Critical About New Feminist Criticism', [review of Katy Deepwell's "New Feminist Art Criticism"], *Women's Art Magazine,* no.67, (November – December 1995), 30-32.
- 'Racial Assault At Aim Gallery Middlesborough', *Bazaar,* no.2, (Summer 1987), 7-8.
- Alistair Raphael, 'Memory's Projections: Synapse at the Photographer's Gallery', *Creative Camera,* no.322, (June – July 1993), 48.
- Clare Rendell, 'The Issue of Painting', *Women Artists Slide Library Journal,* no.13, 3-5.
- Moira Roth, 'The Imprinted Spaces of Sutapa Biswas', in *New Feminist Art Criticism: Critical Strategies,* edited by Katy Deepwell, (Manchester: Manchester University Press, 1995), pp.31-43.
- Gilane Tawadros, 'Beyond the Boundary: Three Black Women Artists', *Third Text,* (Autumn – Winter 1989), 121-150.
- Gilane Tawadros, 'Sutapa Biswas: Remembrance of Things Past and Present', *Third Text,* no.22, (Spring 1993), 47-52.
- Yasmin Yureshin, 'Reworking Myths: Sutapa Biswas', (interview), in *Visibly Female, Feminism And Art: An Anthology,* edited by Hilary Robinson, (London: Camden Press, 1987), pp.37, (Originally published in *Spare Rib,* December 1986).

Black Audio Film Collective
est.1981, (see also John Akomfrah, Eddie George and Trevor Mathison)
Group exhibitions:
1986 *From Two Worlds,* see Chronology.
1990 *The British Art Show,* see Chronology.
Reviews, articles, texts, etc.:
- Reece Auguiste, 'Handsworth Songs: Some Background Notes', *Framework,* no.5, (1988), 4-8.
- Black Audio Film Collective, 'Expedition: Extracts from a Tape-slide Text in Two Parts', *Screen,* 26, no.3/4, (1985), 157-165.
- Sean Cubitt, 'Testament' [review], *Artrage,* no.26, (Autumn 1989), 16.
- Coco Fusco, 'An Interview with Black Audio Film Collective: John Akomfrah, Lina Gopaul, Avril Johnson and Reece Auguiste', in *Young British and Black,* (Buffalo, NY: Hallwalls/Contemporary Arts Center, 1988), pp.41-60.
- Chenaii A. Fyle, 'Black Cinema in Britain: What Way Forward', [interview with David Lawson, Black Audio Film Collective], *Artrage,* (September 1994), 38-39.
- Paul Gilroy & Jim Pines, 'Handsworth Songs: Audiences/Aesthetics/Independence' [interview with the Black Audio Film Collective], *Framework,* no.5, (1988), 9-20.
- 'The Magnificent Seven', *Artrage,* no.26, (Autumn 1989), 16.
- Rukhshana Mosam, 'Who Needs a Heart' [review: Black Audio Film Collective], *Bazaar,* (Spring 1992), 27.
- Julian Petley, '"Testament" and "Possessed by Memory"', [interview with members of the Black Audio Film Collective], *BFI Monthly Film Bulletin,* (September 1989), 259-261.

Bolton, Sylbert Cleve
b.1959, Jamaica.
Group exhibitions:
1984 *Into the Open: New Painting, Prints and Sculpture by Contemporary Black Artists,*
see Chronology.
1987 *Creation For Liberation Open Exhibition,* see Chronology.
1992 *The Dub Factor,* see Chronology.

Bowling, Frank
b.1936, Essequibe, Guyana.
Solo exhibitions:
1977 *Frank Bowling: selected paintings 1967 – 1977,* Acme Gallery.
1986 *Frank Bowling: Paintings 1983 – 1986,* Serpentine Gallery, [Arts Council of Great Britain],
London.
1988 *Frank Bowling,* Castlefield Gallery, Manchester.
1994 *Frank Bowling,* The Cut Gallery, London, (text by Dennis de Caires).
Group exhibitions:
1986 *Caribbean Expressions in Britain,* see Chronology.
1989 *The Other Story,* see Chronology.
1992 *The Dub Factor,* see Chronology.
1995 *The Caribbean Connection,* see Chronology.
Reviews, articles, texts, etc.:
_ *'Frank Bowling' Black Arts in London,* no.138, (August 1991), 28.
_ 'Frank Bowling on Tour', *Artrage,* no.20, (Summer 1988), 32.
_ Peggy Cyphers, 'Frank Bowling' [Tibor de Nagy Gallery, New York; exhibition],
Arts Magazine, (October 1989), 106.
_ Peter Davies, 'Frank Bowling' [Serpentine Gallery, London; exhibition], *Arts Review,*
(14 March 1986), 132-133.
_ Peter Davies, 'Abstract Art in Britain Today' [Serpentine Gallery, London: exhibition],
Art & Artists, no.236, (May 1986), 18-21.
_ Martin Gayford, 'Frank Bowling', *Modern Painters,* (Autumn 1995), 100-101.
_ Mel Gooding, 'Grace Abounding: Bowling's Progress', *Third Text,* no.31, (Summer 1995), 37-46.
_ Gerrit Henry, 'Frank Bowling' [Tibor de Nagy Gallery, New York; exhibition], *Art in America,*
(October 1986), 165.
_ Ian Hunt, 'Frank Bowling', *Art Monthly,* no.192, (December 1995 – January 1996), 39-40.
_ Barbara A.Wolanin, 'Frank Bowling' [National Academy of Sciences, Washington D.C.],
Art in America, (November 1993), 135.

Boyce, Sonia
b.1962, London, England.
Solo exhibitions:
1987 *Sonia Boyce,* Air Gallery, London.
1988 *Sonia Boyce: Recent Work,* Whitechapel Art Gallery, New Gallery, London.
1995 *Sonia Boyce: Peep,* Royal Pavilion Art Gallery, Brighton, [inIVA: London].
Group exhibitions:
1983 *5 Black Women,* see Chronology.
1984 *Into the Open: New Painting, Prints and Sculpture by Contemporary Black Artists*,
see Chronology.
1985 *Black Skin/Bluecoat,* see Chronology.
1985 *Room at the Top,* Nicola Jacobs Gallery, London.

1986 *Caribbean Expressions in Britain*, see Chronology.
1986 *From Two Worlds*, see Chronology.
1986 *Unrecorded Truths*, see Chronology.
1987 *Critical Realism: Britain in the1980's through the Work of 28 artists*, see Chronology.
1987 *State of the Art*, see Chronology.
1987 *The Image Employed: The Use of Narrative in Black Art*, see Chronology.
1988 *The Essential Black Art*, see Chronology.
1988 *The Impossible Self*, Art Gallery, Winnipeg.
1989 *The Other Story*, see Chronology.
1990 *Approaches to Realism*, Bluecoat Gallery, Liverpool.
1990 *The British Art Show*, see Chronology.
1990 *"Distinguishing Marks"*, see Chronology.
1990 *The Invisible City: The London Project II*, The Photographers' Gallery, London.
1991 *Black Markets*, see Chronology.
1991 *Delfina Studios Trust: Catalogue for 1990 and 1991*, Delfina Trust, London.
1991 *Shocks to the System: Social and Political Issues in Recent British Art from the Arts Council Collection*, see Chronology.
1992 *Northern Adventures: an Exhibition of North European Art on Two Sites*, Camden Arts Centre, London.
1992 *White Noise*, see Chronology.
1995 *Cottage Industry*, Beaconsfield, London.
1995 *Fetishism: Visualising Power and Desire*, Royal Pavilion Art Gallery, Brighton.
1995 *Original*, see Chronology.
1995 *Mirage: Enigmas of Race, Difference and Desire*, see Chronology.
1995 *Portable Fabric Shelters*, London Printworks Trust, London.
1995 *Sonia Boyce, Kary Kwok, Alistair Raphael: Free Stories*, L.A.Galerie, Frankfurt, (1 folded leaf).

Texts by Sonia Boyce
1987 John Roberts, 'Interview with Sonia Boyce', *Third Text*, no.1, (Autumn 1987), 55-64.
1988 Sonia Boyce, 'Talking in Tongues', in *Storms of the Heart*, edited by Kwesi Owusu, (London: Camden Press, 1988), pp.219-224.
1995 *Veronica Ryan: Compartments/Apart-ments*, (facsimile of letter by Sonia Boyce), see artist's listing.

Reviews, articles, etc.:
_ Michael Archer, [AIR Gallery, London; exhibition], *Artforum*, (March 1987), 144.
_ Fionna Barber, 'Sonia Boyce: Octagon Gallery, Belfast', *Circa*, no.34 (May – June 1987), 41-43.
_ Mary Rose Beaumont, [AIR Gallery, London; exhibition], *Arts Review*, (16 January 1987), 11-12.
_ 'Sonia Boyce: Recent Work', *Black Arts in London*, no.99, (1 – 15 June 1988), 7.
_ Louisa Buck, 'Sonia Boyce's Recent Work', *City Limits*, (9 – 16 June 1987), 70.
_ Whitney Chadwick, *Women, Art and Society*, (London: Thames & Hudson, 1990), pp.365.
_ Michael Corris, [Vanessa Devereux Gallery, London; exhibition], *Artforum*, (March 1992), 124.
_ Ben Eastop, 'Portable Fabric Shelters' (interview with the curator, Stewart Russell), *everything*, no.17, (1995), 4-6.
_ *Employing The Image: Making Space For Ourselves*, directed by Amanda Holiday, (London, 1989), (video).
_ Genevieve Fox, 'Invisible City' [The Photographer's Gallery, London: exhibit], *Art Monthly*, (December 1990 – January 1991), 24-25.
_ Liam Gillick, 'Wish you Were Here' [Burbage House, London; exhibit], *Art Monthly*, no.180, (October 1994), 38-39.
_ Lorraine Griffiths, 'Home Comforts – Sonia Boyce' [Air Gallery, London; exhibition], *Women Artists Slide Library Journal*, (June – July 1987), 13.
_ Charles Hall, [Vanessa Devereux Gallery; Photographers' Gallery, London; exhibitions], *Arts Review*, (29 November 1991), 603.

- Clare Henry, 'Review of Sonia Boyce Show at the Third Eye Centre' [exhibition from the Air Gallery, London], *Arts Review,* (13 March 1987), 142-143.
- 'Invisible City', *Black Arts in London,* no.130, (1 – 20 November 1990), 6.
- Sarah Kent, 'Review of Air Gallery show', *Time Out,* (17 – 31 December 1986), 35.
- David Lee, 'Sonia Boyce', *Arts Review,* (26 September 1986), 509, (Review of "Conversations" at the Black Art Gallery, London, September – October 1986).
- John Roberts, 'Painting and Sexual Difference' in *Postmodernism, Politics and Art,* (Manchester: Manchester University Press, 1990), pp.178-180.
- Amanda Sebestyen, 'Sonia Boyce: Recent Work', *Women Artists Slide Library Journal,* no.24, (August – September 1988), 27.
- Gilane Tawadros, 'Beyond the Boundary: Three Black Women Artists', *Third Text,* no.8/9, (Autumn – Winter, 1989), 121-150.
- Godfrey Worsdale, 'Portable Fabric Shelters', *Art Monthly,* no.187, (June 1995), 41-42.

Bramble, Chris
b.1958, London, England.
Group exhibitions:
1987 *Creation for Liberation Open Exhibition,* see Chronology.
1990 *"Let the Canvas Come to Life With Dark Faces",* see Chronology.

Brown, Donald
b.1963, Dudley, England.
Group exhibitions:
1988 *Black Art: Plotting the Course,* see Chronology.
1990 *"Let the Canvas Come to Life With Dark Faces",* see Chronology.

Brown, Val
b.1966, England.
Group exhibitions:
1988 *Black Art: Plotting the Course,* see Chronology.
1991 *Four x 4,* see Chronology.
Reviews, articles, texts, etc.:
'Section Three: Portfolio – Val Brown', in *Passion,* edited by Maud Sulter, (Hebden Bridge: Urban Fox Press, 1990).

Burke, Vanley
b.1951, Jamaica.
Solo exhibitions:
[n.d.] *Handsworth from Inside: An Exhibition of Photographs by Vanley Burke,* Bhownagree Gallery, Commonwealth Institute, London.
Group exhibitions:
1983 *Heart in Exile,* see Chronology.
1986 *Connections: Six Artists Linking Two Cities,* Cornerhouse Manchester.
1986 *Reflections of the Black Experience,* see Chronology.
1993 *The Journey,* Watershed Media Centre, Bristol, (publicity material).
1996 *From Negative Image to Positive Stereotype,* see Chronology.
Reviews, articles, texts, etc.:
- Michael Cadette, 'Playing with the Edge: Vanley Burke, the Book', *Creative Camera,*

no.324, (October – November 1993), 46-47.
_ Sue Grayson Ford, 'Connections', *Creative Camera*, no.254, (February 1986), 14.
_ Peter Hagerty, 'Do Commissions Dictate Style?', *Creative Camera*, no.10, (1986), 3.
_ Richard Hylton, 'The Diaspora Experience', *Creative Camera*, no.324, (October – November 1993), 47.
_ Murdoch Lothian, 'Connections', *Ten.8*, no.23, (1986), 42-43.
_ *Vanley Burke: a Retrospective*, edited by Mark Sealy, (London: Lawrence & Wishart, 1993).

Burman, Chila Kumari
b.1958, Liverpool, England.
Solo exhibitions:
1989 *Chila Kumari Burman*, One Spirit Gallery, London.
1990 *Chila Kumari Burman*, Horizon Gallery, London, [Miscellaneous papers].
Group exhibitions:
1985 *3rd Creation for Liberation*, see Chronology.
1985 *GLC Anti-Racist Mural Project 1985*, see Chronology.
1985 *Mirror Reflecting Darkly*, see Chronology.
1985 *The Thin Black Line*, see Chronology.
1986 *The Colours of Black*, see Chronology.
1986 *Twelve Days at the Roundhouse: Mural Artists*, The Roundhouse, London.
1986 *Jagrati*, see Chronology.
1987 *Creation for Liberation Open Exhibition*, see Chronology.
1987 *The Devils Feast*, see Chronology.
1987 *The Image Employed: The Use of Narrative In Black Art*, see Chronology.
1988 *Along the Lines of Resistance: An Exhibition of Contemporary Feminist Art*, see Chronology.
1988 *The Medium and the Message: Five Women Printmakers*, Rochdale Art Gallery.
1988 *Numaish Lalit Kala*, see Chronology.
1989 *Animal Liberation: the Centre of the Circle*, Rochdale Art Gallery.
1989 *Fabled Territories*, see Chronology.
1990 *In Focus*, see Chronology.
1990 *"Let the Canvas Come to Life with Dark Faces"*, see Chronology.
1992 *The Circular Dance*, see Chronology.
1992 *Fine Material for a Dream…? A Reappraisal of Orientalism*, see Chronology.
1992 *Confrontations*, see Chronology.
1993 *Transitions of Riches*, see Chronology.
1994 *With Your Own Face On*, see Chronology.
1994 *Quinta Bienal de la Habana*, see Chronology.
Texts by Chila Kumari Burman:
1987 Chila Kumari Burman and Bhajan Hunjan, 'Mash it up', in *Framing Feminism: Art and the Women's Movement 1970 – 1985*, edited by Roszika Parker & Griselda Pollock, (London: Pandora, 1987), pp.326-330.
1987 Chila Kumari Burman, 'There Have Always Been Great Blackwomen Artists' in *Visibly Female, Feminism and Art: An Anthology*, edited by Hilary Robinson, (London: Camden Press, 1987).
1990 Chila Kumari Burman, 'Ask How I Feel', *FAN-Feminist Art News*, 3, no.6, 16-17.
1990 Chila Burman, 'Automatic Rap: Chila Kumari Burman', *FAN-Feminist Art News*, 3, no.6, 2.
1990 Chila Kumari Burman, 'Don't Rush Me, Hiya Sisters and Hey Mr. Big Stuff', in *Passion*, edited by Maud Sulter, (Hebden Bridge: Urban Fox Press, 1990), pp.53-56.
1992 Chila Kumari Burman, 'Ask How I Feel/Automatic Rap/My New Work', *Third Text*, no.19, (Summer 1992), 79-86.

1994 Chila Kumari Burman, [An Artists Page], *Versus,* no.1, (January – April 1994), 39.
1995 Chila Kumari Burman: [Artists' Pages] in *Let's Get it On: the Politics of Black Performance,* edited by Catherine Ugwu, (London: Institute of Contemporary Arts, 1995), pp.113-117.
Reviews, articles, etc.:
– Allan de Souza, 'Chila Kumari Burman at the One Spirit Gallery', *Bazaar,* no.7, (1989), 23-24.
– Allan de Souza, 'One Spirit Gallery', *Artrage,* no.24, (Spring 1989), 8.
– *Signs Of Resistance,* 1985, see Chronology.
– Tania Guha, 'Chila Kuamri Burman', *Time Out,* (20 – 27 September 1995), 49.
– Hiroko Hagiwara, 'Chila Kumari Burman', *FAN-Feminist Art News,* 3, no.1, (Summer 1989), 28-29.
– 'Identikit: Chila Kumari Burman', *Bazaar,* no.15, 11-13.
– Errol Lloyd, 'Chila Kumari Burman', *Artrage,* no.11, (1986), 15-17. [Interview at the time of the Southall GLC Anti-Racist mural]
– Lynda Nead, *Chila Kumari Burman: Beyond Two Cultures,* (London: Kala Press, 1995), (introduction by Sonali Fernando).
– 'One Spirit Gallery', *Black Arts in London,* no.112, (1 – 31 March 1989), 12.
– Nina Perez, 'Chila Kumari Burman: Horizon Gallery', *FAN-Feminist Art News,* 3, no.6, (1990), 30-31.
– Nina Perez, 'Chila Kumari Burman', *Women's Art Magazine,* no.36, (September – October 1990), 26-27.
– Amanda Sebesteyn, 'Evidence to the Point', *Women's Art Magazine,* no.67, (November – December 1995), 26-27.

Butt, Hamad
b.1962, Lahore, Pakistan; died 1994.
Group exhibitions:
1995 *Rites of Passage,* see Chronology.
Reviews, articles, texts, etc.:
– Stuart Morgan, 'Art au Lait', *Art Monthly,* no.156, (May 1992), 3-5.
– Clement Page, 'Hamad Butt: The Art of Metachemics', *Third Text,* no.32, (Autumn 1995), 33-42.
– Stuart Morgan, 'Hamad Butt' [Milch Gallery, London; exhibition], *Frieze,* (May 1994), 58.

Caesar, Pogus
b.1953, St. Kitts.
Group exhibitions:
1983 *Heart in Exile,* see Chronology.
1984 *Into the Open: New Painting, Prints and Sculpture by Contemporary Black Artists,* see Chronology.
1985 *3rd Creation for Liberation,* see Chronology.
1986 *Caribbean Expressions in Britain,* see Chronology.

Camp, Sokari Douglas
b.1958, Buguma, Nigeria.
Solo exhibitions:
1985 *Sokari Douglas-Camp: Alali,* Ikon Gallery, Birmingham.
1988 *Echoes of the Kalabari: sculpture by Sokari Douglas Camp,* National Museum of African Art, (The Smithsonian Institute) Washington.
1991 *Sokari Douglas Camp: new work,* Sue Williams Gallery, London.
1995 *Play and Display,* Museum of Mankind, London.

Group exhibitions:
1985 *New Horizons,* see Chronology.
1986 *Conceptual Clothing,* see Chronology.
1986 *From Two Worlds,* see Chronology.
1988 *Influences,* see Chronology.
1989 *Time & Motion,* Laing Art Gallery, Newcastle-Upon-Tyne.
1991 *Art for Amnesty: A Contemporary Art Auction,* Bonhams, London.
Reviews, articles, texts, etc.:
 _ 'Sokari Douglas Camp', *Art in America,* (October 1991), 109.
 _ 'Sokari Douglas Camp: Sacred Myths and Pagan Ceremonies', *Revue Noire,* no.2, (September 1991), 30-42, (Interview).
 _ Janice Cheddie, 'Native Informer?', *Women's Art Magazine,* no.67, (November – December 1995), 23-24.
 _ Elsbeth Court, 'Pachipamwe II: the Avant Garde in Africa?', (workshop held in the Cyrene Mission, Zimbabwe), *African Arts,* (January 1992), 38-49.
 _ Dennis Duerden, 'Tradition in Transition: Sokari Douglas Camp', *Contemporary Art,* 3, no.2, (Spring 1996), 68-69.
 _ Lorraine Griffiths, 'Sekiapu: Sokari Douglas-Camp' [Africa Centre, London; exhibition], *Women Artists Slide Library Journal,* (October – November 1987), 20.
 _ W.E.Johnson, 'Sokari Douglas-Camp' [Dorman Memorial Museum, Middlesborough; exhibition], *Arts Review,* (25 September 1987), 646-647.
 _ Christine Mullen Kreamer, 'Echoes of the Kalabari: Sculpture by Sokari Douglas Camp', *African Arts,* (November 1989), 86-87.
 _ Kobena Mercer, 'Art of Africa', *AN-Artists Newsletter,* (December 1995), 28-30.
 _ Simon Njami, 'Sokari Douglas Camp', *Kunstforum International,* no.122, 250-253.

Caur, Arpana
b.1954, New Dehli, India.
Group exhibtions:
1988 *Graven Images,* see Chronology.
1988 *Numaish Lalit Kala,* see Chronology.
1992 *Crossing Black Waters,* see Chronology.
1995 *Inside Out: Contemporary Women Artists of India,* Middlesbrough Art Gallery.
Reviews, articles, texts, etc.:
 _ Eddie Chambers, 'Inside Out: Contemporary Women Artists of India', *Art Monthly,* no.193, (February 1996), 35-37.
 _ Allan de Souza, 'Graven Images – Art, Religion & Politics', *Bazaar,* no.5, (Summer 1988), 21-22, (Preston, Harris Gallery, April – May 1988).
 _ Amal Ghosh, 'Arpana Caur at the October Gallery', *Bazaar,* no.4, (1988), 17.
 _ Peter Gwyn, [October Gallery, London; exhibition], *Arts Review,* (20 November 1987), 803.
 _ Prafulla Mohanti, 'Magical Melancholy: Arpana Caur', [October Gallery, London; exhibition], *Artrage,* no.19, (1988), 12-13.

Chambers, Eddie
b.1960, Wolverhampton, England.
Solo exhibitions:
1984 *Breaking that Bondage/Plotting that Course; 2 Exhibitions by Eddie A.Chambers,* Black Art Gallery, London.
1985 *The Slaughter Of Another Golden Calf: An Exhibition by Eddie Chambers,* Grapevine Arts Centre, Dublin; Bhownagree Gallery, Commonwealth Institute, London.

1985 *The Black Bastard As A Cultural Icon: An Exhibition by Eddie Chambers,* Transmission, Glasgow, 1985; Bookspace, Royal Festival Hall, London, 1986.

Group exhibitions:

1982 *The Pan-Afrikan Connection an Exhibition of Work by Young Black Artists – Good Ideals,* see Chronology.
1983 *The Pan-Afrikan Connection,* see Chronology.
1983 *Heart in Exile,* see Chronology.
1984 *An Exhibition of Radical Black Art by The Blk Art Group,* see Chronology.
1984 *Into the Open: New Painting, Prints and Sculpture by Contemporary Black Artists,* see Chronology.
1985 *Black Skin/Bluecoat,* see Chronology.
1985 *3rd Creation for Liberation,* see Chronology.
1987 *OBAALA's Marcus Garvey Centenary Show,* see Chronology.
1987 *Creation For Liberation Open Exhibition,* see Chronology.
1987 *The Image Employed: the Use of Narrative in Black Art,* see Chronology.
1988 *The Essential Black Art,* see Chronology.
1989 *The Other Story,* see Chronology.

Catalogues of exhibitions curated by Eddie Chambers:

1987 *D-Max,* see Chronology.
1988 *Black Art: Plotting the Course,* see Chronology.
1989 *The Artist Abroad,* see Chronology.
1990 *"Let the Canvas Come to Life with Dark Faces",* see Chronology.
1990 *Diverse cultures,* a Crafts Council touring exhibition.
1991 *Four x 4,* see Chronology.
1991 *Encounters,* Usher Gallery, Lincoln.
1991 *History and Identity,* see Chronology.
1992 *The Dub Factor,* see Chronology.
1993 *Black People and the British Flag,* see Chronology.
1993 *Eugene Palmer,* see artist's listing.
1994 *These Colours Run: Lesley Sanderson,* see artist's listing.
1994 *True Colours: Aboriginal and Torres Strait Islander Artists Raise the Flag,* (London: Eddie Chambers, inIVA; Boomalli Aboriginal Artists Co-operative, Sydney, 1994).
1994 *Michael Platt,* Leicester City Art Gallery.
1994 *Us an' Dem,* see Chronology.
1995 *Phaophanit & Piper,* see Chronology.

Articles by Eddie Chambers:

1985 Eddie Chambers, 'Beyond Ethnic Arts', *Circa,* no.21, (March – April 1985), 6-9.
1985 Eddie Chambers, 'ARTOON-Q-A', *And-Journal of Art and Art Education,* no.7.
1987 Eddie Chambers, 'Talkback', *Creative Camera,* no.5, 38-39.
1988 Eddie Chambers and Juginder Lamba, *The Artpack: A History of Black Artists in Britain,* (London: Haringey Arts Council, 1988).
1988 Eddie Chambers, 'Destruction of the NF', *Third Text,* no.5, (Winter 1988 – 89), 45-49.
1989 Eddie Chambers '…on *Makonde'* [correspondence], *Art Monthly,* no.132, (December 1988 – January 1989), 46.
[n.d.] Eddie Chambers, 'Blackness as Cultural Ikon', *Ten.8: Critical Decade,* 2, no.3, 122-127.
1991 Eddie Chambers, 'Black Markets', *Art Monthly,* no.148, (July – August 1991), 31-33.
1992 Eddie Chambers, 'Alfredo Jaar', *Art Monthly,* no.155, (April 1992), 19. (subsequent correspondence: Elizabeth Macgregor, 'The Ikon Responds', no.156, May 1992, 30).
1992 Eddie Chambers, 'Chambers' Replies', *Art Monthly,* no.157, (June 1992), 28.
1992 Eddie Chambers, 'Trophies of Empire', *Art Monthly,* no.162, (December 1992 – January 1993), 13-15.
1993 Eddie Chambers, 'Bashir Makhoul', *Art Monthly,* no.168, (July – August 1993), 26-27.

1994 Eddie Chambers, 'True Colours', *Versus,* no.2, (1994), 28-29.
1995 Eddie Chambers, 'Who Needs it?' [book review: *Global Visions*], *Art Monthly,* no.83, (February 1995), 45.
1995 Petrine Archer-Straw, 'Eddie Chambers: an Interview', *Art & Design,* [British Art: Defining the Nineties], 10, no.3/4, (March – April 1995), 48-57.
Reviews, texts, etc.:
  – Margaret Garlake, 'Eddie Chambers', *Art Monthly,* (October 1985), 12-13. [Review of "The Black Bastard as a Cultural Icon" at the Pentonville Gallery, 14 September – 6 October 1985].
  – 'Golly Bashing',*Third World First Newsletter,* [n.d.], (Review of "The Black Bastard as a Cultural Icon").
  – Nigel Pollitt, 'Review of "Breaking that Bondage…"' *City Limits,* (16 – 22 November 1984), 65.
  – Nigel Pollitt, 'Review of "The Black Bastard as a Cultural Icon"', *City Limits,* (27 September – 3 October 1985).
  – Cynthia Rose, 'Out of Dark into Light: Cynthia Rose Meets the Founder of Britain's only Black Artists' Archive', *Observer,* (7 October 1990).

Chandra, Avinash
b.1931, Simla, India; died 1991.
Solo exhibitions:
1987 *Avinash Chandra,* Horizon Gallery, London.
Group exhibitions:
1987 *The Other Story*, see Chronology.
Reviews, articles, texts, etc.:
  – Rasheed Araeen, 'Conversation with Avinash Chandra', *Third Text,* no.3/4, (Spring – Summer 1988), 69-95.
  – 'Avinash Chandra', *Third Text,* no.16/17, (Autumn – Winter 1991), 3-4.
  – James Burr, 'Obituary', *Apollo,* no.135, (January 1992), 54.

Chen, Gang
b.1961, China.
Group exhibitions:
1993 *John Moores Liverpool Exhibition 17,* Walker Art Gallery, Liverpool.
1994 *Summer Exhibition,* Delfina Studios, London.
1995 *Journeys West*, see Chronology.

Chuhan, Jagjit
b.1955, India.
Solo exhibitions:
1986 *Secret Spaces: Paintings and Drawings by Jagjit Chuhan,* Rochdale Art Gallery.
1987 *An Exhibition of Paintings And Drawings By Jagjit Chuhan,* Bhownagree Gallery, Commonwealth Institute, London.
Group exhibitions:
1988 *Numaish Lalit Kala,* see Chronology.
1990 *In Focus,* Horizon Gallery, see Chronology.
1990 *New North: New Art from the North of Britain,* see Chronology.
1992 *The Circular Dance,* see Chronology.
1993 *Reclaiming the Madonna: Artists as Mothers,* see Chronology.
1993 *Transition of Riches,* see Chronology.

Reviews, articles, texts, etc.:
_ Sabita Banerji, 'Voluptuous Gardens', *Artrage*, no.18, (Autumn 1987), 44, (Review of Horizon Gallery Show, London, 1987).
_ Mark Currah, 'Horizon: Jagjit Chuhan', *City Limits*, (29 October – 5 November 1987), 71.
_ Jane Sillis, 'Secret Spaces: Paintings and Drawings by Jagjit Chuhan', *Women Artists Slide Library Journal*, (December 1987 – January 1988), 21-22.

Comrie, Jennifer
b.1964, Leeds, England.
Solo exhibitions:
1986 *Carnival Exhibition: Jennifer Comrie*, St.Paul's Gallery, Leeds, (press release).
1987 *Art in Action – The Leeds Residencies*, St.Paul's Gallery, Leeds.
Group exhibitions:
1985 *The Thin Black Line*, see Chronology.
1985 *Mirror Reflecting Darkly*, see Chronology.
1986 *Brushes with the West*, see Chronology.
1987 *The Devils Feast*, see Chronology.
1987 *The Image Employed: the Use of Narrative in Black Art*, see Chronology.

Cooper, Margaret
b.1951, Jamaica.
Group exhibitions:
1985 *3rd Creation for Liberation*, see Chronology.
1985 *New Horizons*, see Chronology.
1987 *Creation for Liberation Open Exhibition*, see Chronology.

Das, Prodeepta
b.1948, Orissa, SE India.
Solo exhibitions:
1987 *The Hill of Flutes: Images from Orissa by Prodeepta Das*, Camerawork, London, (press release and poster).
Group exhibition:
1990 *In Focus*, see Chronology.

Daley, Anthony
b.1960, Jamaica.
Solo exhibitions:
1992 *Anthony Daley*, Flowers East, London.
Group exhibitions:
1989 *Black Art: New Directions*, see Chronology.
1987 *16 Artists: Process & Product*, Turnpike Gallery, Greater Manchester, [Angela Flowers Gallery, London].
1992 *The Dub Factor*, see Chronology.

de Souza, Allan
b.1958, Nairobi, Kenya.

Group exhibitions:
1986 *Brushes with the West,* see Chronology.
1986 *Unrecorded Truths,* see Chronology.
1987 *The Devils Feast,* see Chronology.
1987 *The Image Employed: the Use of Narrative in Black Art,* see Chronology.
1988 *The Essential Black Art,* see Chronology.
1988 *Against The Clause,* Community Copyart, London.
1989 *Fabled Territories,* see Chronology.
1990 *In Focus,* see Chronology.
1990 *"Distinguishing Marks",* see Chronology.
1990 *Autoportraits,* see Chronology.
1990 *"Let The Canvas Come To Life With Dark Faces",* see Chronology.
1991 *Interrogating Identity,* see Chronology.
1992 *Crossing Black Waters,* see Chronology.

Texts by Allan de Souza:
1989 Allan de Souza, 'Cuba Libre: The 1989 Havana Biennale', *Bazaar,* no.11, 12-13.
1988 Allan de Souza, 'Claustrophobia', *Artrage,* no.22/23 (Winter 1988), 4-5.
1987 Allan de Souza, 'Portrait of the Artist as a Dirty Young Man: Text and Images', *Bazaar,*
     no.3, (Winter 1987), 12-13, [reprinted in *Ecstatic Antibodies: Resisting the Aids Mythology,*
     edited by Tessa Boffin and Sunil Gupta, (London: Rivers Oram Press, 1990), pp.64-71].
1994 Allan de Souza, 'Replacing Angels: Extracts and Extractions', in *Tracing Cultures:*
     Art History, Criticism, Critical Fiction, Whitney Museum of American Art, New York, pp.29-51.
1993 Allan de Souza, 'The Spoken Word: Theresa Hak Kyung Cha's *Dictee*', *Third Text,* no.24,
     (Autumn 1993), 73-79.
1990 *Ecstatic Antibodies: Resisting the Aids Mythology,* edited by Tessa Boffin and Sunil Gupta,
     (London: Rivers Oram Press 1990), pp.64-71.

Reviews, articles, etc.:
– Manick Govinda, 'Against the Clause Exhibition', *Bazaar,* no.5, (Summer 1988), 20-21,
  [Community Copyart, London, 1988].
– *Employing the Image: Making Spaces for Ourselves,* directed by Amanda Holiday, 1989,
  London, (video).
– 'Ecstatic Antibodies: Resisting the Aids Mythology', *Black Arts in London,* no.133,
  (1 – 28 February 1991), 8, (Battersea Arts Centre, London).

Dedi, Shakka Gyata
b.1954, USA.

Group exhibitions:
1983 *Heart in Exile,* See Chronology.
1984 *Into the Open: New Painting, Prints and Sculpture by Contemporary Black Artists,*
     see Chronology.
1985 *From Generation to Generation, (The Installation),* see Chronology.
1985 *3rd Creation for Liberation,* see Chronology.

Dhanjal, Avtarjeet
b.1939, Dalla, Punjab.
Group exhibitions:
1985 *3rd Creation for Liberation,* see Chronology.
1989 *The Other Story,* see Chronology.
1995 *Freedom,* see Chronology.

Donkor, Godfried
Dates Unavailable.
Reviews, articles, texts, etc.:
- S. Battastaaghi, 'Gods and Demigods', *Artrage,* (December 1993 – January 1994), 32.
- Frederica Brooks, 'Gods and Demi-Gods: Godfried Donkor', *Third Text,* no.26, (Spring 1994), 97-98.
- 'Image and Ideology', *Black Arts in London,* no.130, (1 – 30 November 1990), 5.

Donovan, Horace Opio
b.1959, Jamaica.
Group exhibitions:
1985 *3rd Creation for Liberation,* see Chronology.
1985 *New Horizons,* see Chronology.
1987 *OBAALA's Marcus Garvey Centenary Show,* see Chronology.
1987 *Creation for Liberation Open Exhibition,* see Chronology.
1988 *"Mysteries",* see Chronology.

Edge, Nina
b.1962, England.
Group exhibitions:
1986 *Jagrati,* see Chronology.
1988 *Along the Lines of Resistance,* see Chronology.
1988 *Black Art: Plotting the Course,* see Chronology.
1991 *A Table for Four,* see Chronology.
1992 *Circular Dance,* see Chronology.
1992 *Crossing Black Waters,* see Chronology.
1992 *Fine Material for a Dream…?: A Reappraisal of Orientalism,* see Chronology.
1992 *Trophies of Empire,* see Chronology.
1995 *Mirage,* see Chronology.
Texts by Nina Edge:
1992 Nina Edge, 'Home International', *FAN-Feminist Art News,* 4, no.1. 18-20.
1995 Nina Edge, 'Riding the Time Line', in *Let's Get It On,* edited by Catherine Ugwu, (London: Institute of Contemporary Arts; Seattle: Bay Press, 1995).
1990 Nina Edge, 'Your Name is Mud', in *Passion,* edited by Maud Sulter, (Hebden Bridge: Urban Fox Press, 1990), pp.154-167.
Reviews, articles, etc.:
- Sean Cubitt, 'Nina Edge/Peter Beeton', [Bluecoat Gallery, Liverpool; installations], *Art Monthly,* no.180, (October 1994), 31-33.
- Nina Edge, 'Identikit', *Bazaar,* (Summer 1991), 11-14.
- 'Section Three: Portfolio – Nina Edge', in *Passion,* edited by Maud Sulter, (Hebden Bridge: Urban Fox Press, 1990), pp.214-215

Egonu, Uzo,
b.1931, Onitsha, Nigeria.
Solo exhibitions:
1986 *Uzo Ugonu Now 1986: Stateless People – Exhibition of Paintings, Drawings, & Prints,* Royal Festival Hall, London.
Group exhibitions:
1984 *Into the Open: New Painting, Prints and Sculpture by Contemporary Black Artists,* see Chronology.
1986 *The Colours of Black,* see Chronology.
1986 *Double Vision,* see Chronology.
1989 *The Other Story,* see Chronology.
1990 *"Let the Canvas Come to Life with Dark Faces",* see Chronology.
1994 *Seen|Unseen,* see Chronology.
Reviews, articles, texts, etc.:
– Uzo Egonu, 'African Art: Its Impact on the West', *Arts Review,* (9 November 1984), 558.
– Olu Oguibe, *Uzo Egonu: An African Artist in the West,* (London: Kala Press, 1995).
– Hiltrud Streicher and Uzo Egonu, 'Reflections of Uzo Egonu', *Third Text,* no.8/9, (Autumn – Winter 1989), 173-182.

Fani-Kayode, Rotimi,
b.1955; died 1989, London, England.
Group exhibitions:
1988 *The Invisible Man,* Goldsmith's Gallery, London.
1989 *US/UK Photography Exchange,* Jamaica Arts Center, New York; and Camerawork, London.
1990 *Autoportraits,* see Chronology.
Reviews, articles, texts:
– '198 Gallery', *Black Arts in London,* no.131-132, (16 December 1990 – 31 January 1991), 5.
– 'Abiku – Born to Die', *Black Arts in London,* no.106, (1 – 15 October 1988), 7.
– John Akomfrah, 'On the Borderline', *Ten.8,* 2, no.1, (Spring 1991), 50-67.
– 'Autograph', *Artrage,* no.22/23, (Winter 1988), 29.
– David Bailey, 'Exploring the Photographic Technique of RFK', [from catalogue US/UK Camerawork, London, 1989], *Revue Noire,* no.3, (December 1991), 33-37.
– David A. Bailey, 'Photographic Animateur: the Photographs of Rotimi Fani-Kayode in Relation to Black Photographic Practice', *Third Text,* no.13, (Winter1990 – 1991), 37-62.
– *Bodies of Experience: Stories about Living with HIV,* (London: Camerawork, 1989).
– Emmanuel Cooper, 'On Rotimi Fani-Kayode', *Time Out,* (16 – 23 January 1991), 27.
– Carole Enaharo, 'Rotimi Fani-Kayode', *Artrage,* (Summer 1989), 40.
– *Ecstatic Antibodies,* 1990, see Chronology.
– Rotimi Fani-Kayode, 'Traces Of Ecstasy', *Ten.8,* no.28, 36-43, (reprinted in *Ten.8: Critical Decade,* 2, no.3, (Spring 1992), 64-71.
– Sunil Gupta, 'Photography, Sexuality & Cultural Difference: the Emergence of Black Lesbian and Gay Identities in the UK', "Disputed Identities", *SF Camerawork Quarterly,* 17, no.3, (Fall 1990), 19-26.
– Charles Hall, 'Rotimi Fani-Kayode' [198 Gallery, London; exhibit], *Arts Review,* (25 January 1991).
– Alex Hirst, 'Acts of God', *Revue Noire,* no.3, (December 1991), 38-50.
– Alex Hirst, 'Oluwarotimi Adebiyi Fani-Kayode', [obituary], *Bazaar,* no.11, (1990), 2.
– Rose Jennings, 'Rotimi Fani-Kayode:198 Gallery', *City Limits,* (10 – 17 January 1991), 25.
– Brian Kennedy, 'Out in the city – photography exhibition by Rotimi Fani-Kayode', *City Limits,* (23 – 30 June 1988), 61.
– Kobena Mercer, 'Dark & Lovely: Notes on Black Gay Image Making', *Ten.8,* 2, no.1,

(Spring 1991), 78-86.
_ Mark Reid, 'The Photography of Rotimi Fani-Kayode', *Wide Angle*, 14, no.2, (April 1992), 38-50.
_ Pascal Martin Saint Leon and Jean Loup Pivin, 'Rotimi Fani-Kayode & A. Hirst', *Revue Noire*, no.3, (December 1991), 30-32.
_ 'Transatlantinc Dialogues', *Black Arts in London,* no.119, (1 – 30 November 1989), 10, (Camerawork, London).

Forde, Stephen
b.1968, England.
Group exhibitions:
1991 *Four x 4,* see Chronology.
Artists' book:
1993 *The Phone Box: Art in Telephone Boxes,* (London: Virginia Nimarkoh/Bookworks, 1993), (edition of 300 with original artists works).

Forrester, Denzil
b.1956, Grenada.
Solo exhibitions:
1986 *An Exhibition of Drawings by Denzil Forrester,* Bhownagree Gallery, Commonwealth Institute, London.
1990 *Dub Transition: Denzil Forrester: A Decade of Paintings 1980 – 1990,* Harris Museum and Art Galllery, Preston.
Group exhibitions:
1983 *Germinations 1983 – 1984: Exhibition of Art Students from France, Great Britain and Federal Republic of Germany,* Museum Fridericanium, Kassel.
1983 *Painting and Printmaking Degree Show,* Royal College of Art, London.
1984 *The Image as Catalyst,* McAlpine Gallery, Ashmolean Museum, Oxford.
1986 *Caribbean Expressions in Britain,* see Chronology.
1986 *From Two Worlds,* see Chronology.
1988 *Figuring out the Eighties,* see Chronology.
1992 *The Dub Factor,* see Chronology.
1994 *Us An' Dem: a Critical Look at the Relationships Between the Police, the Judiciary and the Black Community,* see Chronology.
1995 *Farewell to Shadowland,* see Chronology.
1996 *Imagined Communities, 1996 – 1997:* see Chronology.
Reviews, articles, texts, etc.:
_ Mary Rose Beaumont, 'Islington Arts Factory', *Arts Review,* (24 February 1989), 155.
_ Michael Bracewell, 'Beyond These Four Walls,' ("Imagined Communities"), *Independent,* (13 February 1996).
_ 'Denzil Forrester: "Burial of Winston Rose"', *Arts Review,* (26 September 1986), 512.
_ Chris Wadsworth, 'Denzil Forrester', [Gateshead Library Gallery, England], *Arts Review,* (28 July 1989), 566.

Francis, Armet
Dates Unavailable.
Solo exhibitions:
1986 *The Black Triangle: Armet Francis,* Cockpit Gallery, London.
Group exhibitions:
1986 *The Colours of Black,* see Chronology.

1986 *Reflections of the Black Experience,* see Chronology.
Texts by Armet Francis:
1985 Armet Francis, *The Black Triangle: The People of the African Diaspora,* (London: Seed, 1985).
Reviews, articles, etc.:
 _ Anna Arnone, 'Armet Francis', (interview), *City Limits,* (14 – 20 February 1986), 78-79.
 _ David Briers, 'The Black Triangle: People of the African Diaspora',
  (The Ffotogallery, Cardiff, Wales), *Creative Camera,* no.5, (1987), 33.
 _ 'Children of the Black Triangle: an Interview with Armet Francis', in *Storms of the Heart,*
  edited by Kwesi Owusu, (London: Camden Press, 1988), pp.181-190.
 _ 'Exhibition by Armet Francis at the Photographer's Gallery', *Artrage,* no.5, (Autumn 1983), 28.

Fraser-Munro, Ronald
Dates Unavailable.
Group exhibitions:
1995 *Maison Garçon,* [director Rony Phrasre-Monreau], Camerawork, London, (press release).
Reviews, articles, texts, etc.:
 'Artists Pages', in *Let's Get It On: The Politics of Black Performance,*
 edited by Catherine Ugwu, (London: Institute of Contemporary Arts, 1995), pp.118-123.

George, Eddie (see also Black Audio Film Collective)
b.1963, London, England.
Group exhibitions:
1987 *The Image Employed,* see Chronology.
1995 *Mirage,* see Chronology.
Reviews, articles, texts, etc.:
 Eddie George, 'Black Body & Public Enemy', *Ten.8,* 2, no.1, (Spring 1991), 68-77.

Ghosh, Amal
b.1933, Calcutta.
Solo exhibitions:
1987 *Connections: Amal Ghosh,* Horizon Gallery, London.
1995 *Amal Ghosh: Vitreous Enamel Murals,* Treatment Room, Eastman Dental Hospital, London.
Group exhibitions:
1988 *Numaish Lalit Kala,* see Chronology.
1990 *In Focus,* see Chronology.
1993 *Transition of Riches,* see Chronology.
Reviews, articles, texts, etc.:
 _ Michael Horn, 'Amal Ghosh at the Horizon Gallery', September 1987, *Bazaar,* no.3,
  (Winter 1987), 17-18.
 _ Onita Hudson, 'Amal Ghosh' [Horizon Gallery, London; exhibition], *Artrage,* no.18
  (Autumn 1987), 41.

Gregory, Joy
b.1959, Bicester, England.
Group exhibitions:
1987 *Polareyes,* see Chronology.
1990 *Autoportraits,* see Chronology.
1990 *Ecstatic Antibodies,* see Chronology.

1992 *Who Do You Take Me For?,* see Chronology.
1995 *4th Istanbul Biennal 1995,* Istanbul Foundation for Culture and Arts.
Reviews, articles, texts, etc.:
– Joy Gregory, 'Fantasy: Joy Gregory Speaking to Maxine Walker', *Polareyes,* no.1, (1987), 18-19.
– Joy Gregory, in 'Redrawing the Map', *Creative Camera,* no.325,
  (December 1993 – January 1994), 17.
– Joy Gregory, 'Bus Loads of Faith', *Creative Camera,* (June – July 1995), 50, (interview).

Gupta, Sunil
b.1953, New Delhi, India.
Group exhibitions:
1986 *Darshan,* see Chronology.
1986 *Reflections of the Black Experience,* see Chronology.
1989 *Fabled Territories,* see Chronology.
1990 *Post-Morality,* see Chronology.
1990 *Autoportraits,* see Chronology.
1991 *Shocks to the System: Social and Political Issues in Recent British art from the Arts
  Council Collection,* see Chronology.
1992 *Fine Material for a Dream…?: A Reappraisal of Orientalism,* see Chronology.
1992 *Trophies of Empire,* see Chronology.
1992 *Who Do You Take Me For?* see Chronology.
1994 *Quinta Bienal de la Habana,* see Chronology.
Texts by Sunil Gupta:
1986 Sunil Gupta, 'Northern Media, Southern Lives', in *Photography/Politics: Two,*
  edited by Patricia Holland, Jo Spence, and Simon Watney, (London: Comedia, 1986),
  pp.162-166.
1990 *Ecstatic Antibodies: Resisting the Aids Mythology,* edited by Tessa Boffin and Sunil Gupta,
  (London: Rivers Oram Press, 1990).
1990 Sunil Gupta, 'Photography, Sexuality & Cultural Difference: the Emergence of Black
  Lesbian and Gay Identities in the UK', "Disputed Indentities", *SF Camerawork Quarterly,* 17,
  no.3, (Fall 1990), 19-26.
1992 Sunil Gupta, 'At the Crossroads', *Creative Camera,* no.313, (December – January 1992), 19-20.
1992 Sunil Gupta, 'Desire And Black Men', *Ten.8,* no.22, 17-23,
  (reprinted in *Ten.8: Critical Decade,* 2, no.3, (Spring 1992), 80-85).
1994 'Imagining a New Internationalism', Sunil Gupta interviewed by Nikos Papastergiadis,
  Creative Camera, no.327, (April – May 1994), 18-23.
Reviews, articles, etc.:
– 'Ecstatic Antibodies', *Black Arts in London,* no.133, (1 – 28 February 1991), 8.
– Kobena Mercer, 'Dark & Lovely', *Ten.8,* 2, no.1, (Spring 1991), 78-86.

Gutsa, Tapfuma (Moses)
b.1956, Zimbabwe.
Group exhibitions:
1985 *3rd Creation for Liberation,* see Chronology.
1985 *New Horizons,* see Chronology.
Reviews, articles, texts, etc.:
– Elsbeth Court, 'Pachipamwe II: The Avant Garde in Africa?',
  (workshop held in the Cyrene Mission, Zimbabwe), *African Arts,* 25, (January 1992), 38-49.
– Kate Ezra, 'Contemporary African Artists: Changing Tradition',
  (The Studio Museum in Harlem, New York), *African Arts,* 23, (October 1990), 79-80.

_ Tapfuma Gutsa, 'Listening to the Baby Kick', *Arts Review,* (7 September 1990), back cover.
_ David Joselit, 'Africa Rising', *Art in America,* (October 1990), 160-161.
_ Andre Maignan, 'Henry Munyaradzi, Nicholas Mukomberanwa and Tapfuma Gutsa', *Art International,* no.11, (Summer 1990), 88.
_ Grace Stanislaus, 'Frozen Spirit: Zimbabwean Stone Sculpture', *Sculpture,* (January – February 1992), 44-47.

Hammad, Medina
b.1963, England.
Reviews, articles, texts, etc.:
1990 *"Let the Canvas Come to Life with Dark Faces,"* see Chronology.
1991 *Four x 4,* see Chronology.
1991 *History and Identity: Seven Painters,* see Chronology.

Hatoum, Mona
b.1952, Beirut, Lebanon.
Solo exhibitions:
1992 *Dissected Space: New Installations 1990 – 1992,* Chapter Arts Centre, Cardiff.
1993 *Mona Hatoum,* Arnolfini, Bristol.
1994 *Mona Hatoum,* Centre Georges Pompidou, Paris.
Group exhibitions:
1986 *Conceptual Clothing,* see Chronology.
1987 *Dislocations,* see Chronology.
1987 *State of the Nation,* Herbert Gallery & Museum, Coventry.
1988 *Along the Lines of Resistance: An Exhibition of Contemporary Feminist Art,* see Chronology.
1988 *The Essential Black Art,* see Chronology.
1988 *In an Unsafe Light,* Ikon Gallery, Birmingham.
1989 *The Other Story,* see Chronology.
1989 *Intimate Distance,* see Chronology.
1990 *The British Art Show,* see Chronology.
1990 *Disputed Identities,* see Chronology.
1990 *New Works For Different Places: TSWA Four Cities Project,* see Chronology.
1991 *Interrogating Identity,* see Chronology.
1991 *Shocks to the System: Social and Political Issues in Recent British Art from the Arts Council Collection,* see Chronology.
1992 *Brit Art [11 Britische Kunstler],* Kunstverein, Glarus.
1992 *Fine Material for a Dream…?: A Reappraisal of Orientalism,* see Chronology.
1992 *Who do You Take Me for,* see Chronology.
1993 *Andrea Fisher/Mona Hatoum,* South London Gallery, London.
1993 *Four Rooms,* see Chronology.
1994 *Quinta Bienal de la Habana,* see Chronology.
1994 *Sense and Sensibility: Women Artists and Minimalism in the Nineties,* Museum of Modern Art, New York.
1995 *Cocido y Crudo,* see Chronology.
1995 *Freedom,* see Chronology.
1995 *Objects in Advance of the Concept,* Burnaby Art Gallery, Burnaby.
1995 *Rites of Passages,* see Chronology.
Texts, video works, etc by Mona Hatoum:
1983 Mona Hatoum, *So Much I Want to Say,* (video).
1984 Mona Hatoum, *Changing parts,* (video).

[n.d.] Mona Hatoum 'Talking at the Air Gallery, London, about her Installation,
 "Hidden From Prying Eyes"', *Audio Arts Magazine,* 8, no.2/3, Tape 2, Side 2.
1988 Mona Hatoum, *Measures of Distance,* (video).
1994 William Furlong, 'Interview with Mona Hatoum', *Audio Arts Magazine,* 13, no.4,
 (audio-cassette).
Reviews, articles, etc.:
 _ Libby Anson, 'Mona Hatoum', *Art Monthly,* no.184, (March 1995), 31-32.
 _ Michael Archer, 'Mona Hatoum' [Mario Flecha, London; installation], *Artforum,*
  (December 1992), 107-108.
 _ Renee Baert, 'Measures of Distance', *Screen,* 34, (Summer 1993), 111-123.
 _ Laurel Berger, 'In Between, Outside & in the Margins', *Art News,* (September 1994), 148-149.
 _ Tania Guha, 'Andrea Fisher/Mona Hatoum' [South London Gallery, exhibition], *Third Text,*
  no.24, (Autumn 1993), 103-106.
 _ Guy Brett, 'Mona Hatoum' [The Showroom, London; installation], *Art in America,*
  (November 1989), 205.
 _ P. D. Burwell, 'Changing Parts', *High Performance,* 8, no.2, (1985), 91-92.
 _ Dan Cameron, 'Openings', *Artforum,* (April 1993), 92.
 _ Johanna Drucker, 'Sense and Sensibility: Women Artists and Minimalism in the Nineties',
  Third Text, no.27, (Summer 1994), 103-107.
 _ Steven Durland, 'Throwing a Hot Coal in a Bathtub: London's Edge 88'
  (a Biennale of Experimental Art), *High Performance,* (Winter 1988), 32-41, (37-38).
 _ 'Edge 88', *Performance,* no.55, (1988), 38-39, (Edge 88, London Performance Festival,
  13-25 September 1988).
 _ Catherine Elwes, 'Notes from a Video Performance by Mona Hatoum', *Undercut,* no.1,
  (March – April 1981), 28.
 _ Brian Hatton, 'Umspace', *Art Monthly,* no.167, (June 1993), 19-21,
  (*Four Rooms,* Serpentine Gallery, London).
 _ 'Mona Hatoum: "Light Sentence"', *Artforum,* (Summer 1994), 61.
 _ *Issues In Women's Studies: Outside In – Women Artists and Cultural Difference,*
  Programme 7, Open University, Milton Keynes, 1991, (video).
 _ Lynn MacRitchie, 'Report from London: Uneasy Rooms', *Art in America,* (October 1993), 60-61.
 _ Melanie Marino, 'Mona Hatoum at CRG', *Art in America,* (January 1995), 97-98.
 _ Bol Marjoram, 'Mona Hatoum – not an Entertainer', *Performance,* no.41,
  (May – June 1986), 20-23.
 _ Laura U.Marks, 'Sexual Hybrids: From Oriental Exotics to Postcolonial Grotesque',
  Parachute, no.70, (April – June 1993), 22-29.
 _ Desai Philippi, 'The Witness Beside Herself', *Third Text,* no.12, (Autumn 1990), 71-80.
 _ Clare Rendell, 'New Installations, 1990 – 1992', *Arts Review,* (December 1992), 39.
 _ Dot Tuer, 'Perspectives of the Body in Canadian Art', *C Magazine,* no.36, (Winter 1993), 29-37.
 _ Caryn Faure Walker, 'Mona Hatoum', in *Ecstasy, Ecstasy, Ecstasy, She Said,*
  Women's Art in Britain: a Partial View, (Manchester: Cornerhouse, 1994), pp.39-43.
 _ Piers Wilke, 'Mona Hatoum', *Women Artists Slide Library Journal,* no.30, (1990), 28.

Higgins, Kif
Dates Unavailable.
Reviews, articles, texts, etc.:
 'Artists Pages', in *Let's Get it on: The Politics of Black Performance,*
  edited by Catherine Ugwu, (London: Institute of Contemporary Arts, 1995), pp.130-135.

Himid, Lubaina
b.1954, Tanzania.

Solo exhibitions:
1986 *A Fashionable Marriage: a New Installation by Lubaina Himid,* Pentonville Gallery, London.
1989 *The Ballad of the Wing: Installation of Paintings and Sculptures made for Museums Year,*
City Museum and Art Gallery, Stoke-on-Trent; and the Chisenhale Gallery, London.
1992 *Lubaina Himid: Revenge,* Rochdale Art Gallery, Rochdale,
(texts by Jill Morgan and Maud Sulter).

Group exhibitions:
1983 *Five Black Women,* see Chronology.
1984 *Into the Open: New Painting, Prints and Sculpture by Contemporary Black Artists,*
see Chronology.
1985 *Combinations/Lubaina Himid, Jaginder Lamba,* see Chronology.
1985 *Creation for Liberation,* see Chronology.
1985 *GLC Anti-Racist Mural Project,* see Chronology.
1985 *New Horizons,* see Chronology.
1985 *The Thin Black Line,* see Chronology.
1986 *Winter Exhibition,* Blond Fine Art, London.
1986 *From Two Worlds,* see Chronology.
1986 *Twelve Days at the Roundhouse: Mural Artists,* see Chronology.
1987 *Depicting History: For Today,* Mappin Art Gallery, Sheffield.
1987 *New Robes for Mashulan,* see Chronology.
1987 *Palaces of Culture: The Great Museum,* City Museum and Art Gallery, Stoke-on-Trent.
1988 *Along the Lines of Resistance: An Exhibition of Contemporary Feminist Art,* see Chronology.
1988 *Influences,* see Chronology.
1989 *After 1789: Ideas and Images of Revolution,* Kettle's Yard, Cambridge.
1989 *The Other Story,* see Chronology.
1989 *Passion,* see Chronology.
1990 *Heritage, Image and History,* see Chronology.
1990 *Treatise on the Sublime,* see Chronology.
1992 *Columbus Drowning,* see Chronology.
1994 *Quinta Bienal de la Habana,* see Chronology.
1994 *Seen\Unseen,* see Chronology.

Texts by Lubaina Himid:
1989 Lubaina Himid, 'The Wing Museum: The Ballad of the Wing, Museum as Metaphor',
FAN-Feminist Art News, 3, no.1, (Summer 1989), 14-15.
1990 Lubaina Himid, 'The Ballad of the Wing', *And-Journal of Art and Art Education,* no.21, 13-16.
1990 Lubaina Himid, 'Mapping: a Decade of Black Women Artists' in *Passion,*
edited by Maud Sulter, (Hebden Bridge: Urban Fox Press, 1990), pp.63-72.
1990 Lubaina Himid, 'Objects are in most of their more obvious manifestations, subjects',
in *Lotte or the Transformation of the Art Object,* (Graz: Grazer Kunstverien,1990), pp.34-35.
1994 *Maud Sulter: Syrcas,* see artist's listing.
1994 Lubaina Himid, 'A Memorial to Zong', *AN-Artists Newsletter,* (February 1994), 30-31.

Exhibitions curated by Lubaina Himid:
1984 *Into the Open,* see Chronology.
1985 *Thin Black Line,* see Chronology.
1986 *Unrecorded Truths,* see Chronology.
1987 *Out There Fighting,* an Elbow Room Show, London, 1986 – 1987.
1987 *New Robes for MaShulan,* see Chronology.
1987 *State of the Art,* see Chronology.

Reviews, articles, etc.:
_ Whitney Chadwick, *Women, Art and Society,* (London: Thames & Hudson, 1990), pp.364-365.

– Emmanuel Cooper, 'Lubaina Himid – Chisenhale Gallery', *Time Out,* no.988, (26 July – 2 August 1989), 32.
– 'Gold Blooded Warrior: New Work by Lubaina Himid & Maud Sulter', *Black Arts in London,* no.97, (1 – 15 May 1988), 13. (Tom Allen Centre, London).
– *Signs of Resistance,* 1985: see Chronology.
– Delta Streete, 'Revenge by Lubaina Himid', *FAN-Feminist Art News,* 4, no.3, 31-32.
– Gilane Tawadros, 'Beyond the Boundary: Three Black Women Artists', *Third Text,* (Autumn – Winter 1989), 121-150.

Holiday, Amanda
b.1964, Sierra Leone.
Group exhibitions:
1985 *3rd Creation for Liberation,* see Chronology.
1987 *Creation for Liberation Open Exhibition,* see Chronology.
1987 *The Image Employed: The Use of Narrative in Black Art,* see Chroology.
1988 *Black Art: Plotting the Course,* see Chronology.
1988 *Incantations Reclaiming Imagination,* see Chronology.
1989 *Black Art: New Directions,* see Chronology.
Video work:
1989 *Employing The Image: Making Space for Ourselves,* directed by Amanda Holiday, (London).
Reviews, articles, texts, etc.:
– 'Bedford Hill Gallery Presents "Umbrage"', *Black Arts in London,* no.118, (1 – 31 October 1989), 9.
– Hagiwara, Hiroko, 'Between Fear and Fantasy, Amanda Holiday's Film Work', *Women's Art Magazine,* no.44, (January – February 1992), 17.
– Hagiwara Hiroko, 'Breaking through the Showcase; Amanda Holiday's Video, "Employing the Image"', *FAN-Feminist Art News,* 3, no.8, (1991), 28-30.

Holmes, Claudette
b.1962, Place of Birth Unavailable.
Group Exhibitions:
1996 *From Negative Image to Positive Stereotype,* see Chronology.
1990 *In Sight In View,* see Chronology.
Reviews, articles, texts, etc.:
– 'Claudette Holmes', *Black Arts in London,* no.138, (August 1991), 29.
– Claudette Holmes, 'Portfolio', *Blackboard Review,* no.2, (1990), 25-28.

Houshiary, Shirazeh.
b.1955, Shiraz, Iran.
Solo exhibitions:
1984 *Shirazeh Houshiary,* Lisson Gallery, London.
1988 *Shirazeh Houshiary,* Museum of Modern Art, Oxford & Centre d'Art Contemporain, Genève.
1988 *Dancing Around My Ghost,* Camden Arts Centre, London.
1993 *Turning Around the Centre,* University Gallery, University of Massachusetts, Amherst.
1994 *Conversation with Shirazeh Houshiary and Stella Santacatterina,* published on the occasion of an exhibition held at the Lisson Gallery, London, (reprinted from *Third Text,* no.27, Summer 1994).

1995 *Isthmus: Shirazeh Houshiary,* (Grenoble: Magasin-Centre National d'Art Contemporain de Grenoble; London: the British Council).
Group exhibitions:
1983 *New Art at the Tate Gallery,* Tate Gallery, London.
1983 *The Sculpture Show,* Hayward and Serpentine Galleries, London.
1984 *The British Art Show,* Art Council Touring Exhibition.
1985 *The British Show,* Art Gallery of New South Wales, Sydney.
1989 *Magiciens de la Terre,* Centre Georges Pompidou, Paris.
1993 *In Site: New British Sculpture,* Museet for Samtidskunst, Oslo.
1993 *Recent British Sculpture,* City Museum and Art Gallery, Derby.
1994 *The Turner Prize,* Tate Gallery, London.
1994 *Sculptors' Drawings Presented by the Weltkunst Foundation,* see Chronology.
1995 *Contemporary British Art in Print,* Scottish National Gallery, Edinburgh.
Reviews, articles, texts, etc.:
– Michael Corris, 'Shirazeh Houshiary' [Lisson Gallery, London; exhibition], *Artforum,* (November 1992), 121.
– Sasha Craddock, 'In and out of Focus', *Women's Art Magazine,* no.61, (November – December 1994), 22.
– Tony Godfrey, 'Contemporary British Sculpture', *The Burlington Magazine,* 135, (December 1993), 841.
– Charles Hall, 'Shirazeh Houshiary' [Lisson Gallery, London; exhibition], *Arts Review,* (June 1992), 225-226.
– 'Time and Tide: The Tyne International Exhibition of Contemporary Art', *Art & Design Profile,* no.32, (1993), 65-69.
– 'Shirazeh Houshiary', *Art & Design,* 10, no.1/2, (January – February 1995), vi. [The Contemporary Sublime].
– Jeffrey Kastner, 'Shirazeh Houshiary', *Flash Art,* no.80, (January – February 1995), 102.
– Rupert Martin, 'Shirazeh Houshiary' [Lisson Gallery, London; exhibition], *Flash Art,* no.120, (January 1985), 47.
– Ann Barclay Morgan, 'Studio: Shirazeh Houshiary', *Sculpture,* 13, (July – August 1994), 10-11.
– Hilary Robinson, 'Shirazeh Houshiary' [Douglas Hyde Gallery, Dublin; exhibition], *Circa,* no.67, (Spring 1994), 60-61.
– Stella Santacatterina, 'Conversation with Shirazeh Houshiary', *Third Text,* no.27, (Summer 1994), 77-86.
– Pier Luigi Tazzi, 'Seductives Lures: Shirazeh Houshiary', *Artforum,* (Summer 1988), 97-98.
– *The Turner Prize, Without Walls:* Channel Four, London, 1994, (video).

Hunjan, Bhajun
b.1956, Kenya.
Solo exhibitions:
1989 *Bhajan Hunjan: Recent Works,* Horizon Gallery, London.
Group exhibitions:
1986 *Jagrati,* see Chronology.
1990 *In Focus,* see Chronology.
1990 *"Let the Canvas Come to Life with Dark Faces",* see Chronology.
1991 *A Table for Four,* see Chronology.
1992 *Crossing Black Waters,* see Chronology.
1993 *Black People and the British Flag,* see Chronology.
1994 *Divers Memories,* Pitt Rivers Museum, Oxford.
Texts by Bhajan Hunjun:
1987 Chila Kumari Burman and Bhajun Hunjan, 'Mash it Up', in *Framing Feminism:*

Art and the Womens Movement, 1970 – 1985, edited by Roszika Parker
and Griselda Pollock, (London: Pandora, 1987), pp.326-330.
Reviews, articles, etc.:
_ Allan de Souza, 'Bhajan Hunjan', *Bazaar,* no.7, (1989), 23.
_ 'Recent Works by Bhajun Hunjun', *Black Arts in London,* no.111, (1 February – 1 March 1989),
  13. (Horizon Gallery, London).
_ 'Section Three: Portfolio – Bhajun Hunjun', in *Passion,* edited by Maud Sulter,
  (Hebden Bridge: Urban Fox Press, 1990), pp.192-195.
_ Nadir Tharani, 'Bhajan Hunjan', *Artrage,* no.24, (Spring 1989), 11.

Hylton, Richard
b.1967, England.
Group exhibitions:
1990 *"Let the Canvas Come to Life with Dark Faces,"* see Chronology.
1991 *Four x 4,* see Chronology.
1992 *White Noise,* see Chronology.
1993 *Black People and the British Flag,* see Chronology.

Jadunath, Anthony
b.1945, Trinidad.
Group exhibitions:
1985 *3rd Creation for Liberation,* see Chronology.
1985 *New Horizons,* see Chronology.
1986 *Caribbean Expressions in Britain,* see Chronology.
1987 *Creation for Liberation Open Exhibition,* see Chronology.
1988 *Contemporary Art by Afro-Caribbean Artists,* see Chronology.
1990 *"Let the Canvas Come to Life with Dark Faces",* see Chronology.

Janah, Sunil
b.1918, Dibrugarh, Assam.
Group exhibitions:
1986 *Darshan,* see Chronology.
1992 *Fine Material for a Dream…?: A Reappraisal of Orientalism,* see Chronology.
Reviews, articles, texts, etc.:
_ Rabhu Guptara, 'Sunil Janah', *Ten.8,* no.27, (1987), 12-25.
_ Sandip Hazareesingh, 'History Through Photography: an Interview with Sunil Janah',
  Dragon's Teeth, no.26, (Spring 1987), 5-6.
_ Sunil Janah, 'Famine in Rayalseema, South India' (1945), *Art in America,* October 1990), 64.

Jantjes, Gavin
b.1948, Cape Town, South Africa.
Solo exhibitions:
1978 *Gavin Jantjes: Graphic Work 1974 – 1978, Exhibition for the International Anti-Apartheid Year,*
  Kulturhuset, Stockholm.
1984 *Gavin Jantjes: Paintings and Drawings,* Midland Art Group, Nottingham.
1986 *Korabra: Paintings by Gavin Jantjes,* Edward Totah Gallery, London.
Group exhibitions:
1982 *Prophecy and Vision,* Arnolfini, Bristol.

1984 *Into the Open: New Painting, Prints and Sculpture by Contemporary Black Artists,*
see Chronology.
1985 *GLC Anti-Racist Mural Project 1985,* see Chronology.
1986 *The Colours of Black,* see Chronology.
1986 *From Two Worlds,* see Chronology.
1988 *The Essential Black Art,* see Chronology.
1989 *One Spirit: Black Artists Against Racism,* see Chronology.
1989 *The Other Story,* see Chronology.
1991 *Shocks to the System: Social and Political Issues in Recent British Art from the Arts Council Collection,* see Chronology.
1994 *Quinta Bienal de la Habana,* see Chronology.
Texts by Gavin Jantjes:
1978 Gavin Jantjes, *A South African Colouring Book: 1974 – 1975,* (Geneva: Gavin Jantjes, 1978), [Fascimile ed.]
1988 Gavin Jantjes, 'Korabra', in *Storms of the Heart,* edited by Kwesi Owusu, (London: Camden Press, 1988), pp.253-262.
1989 Gavin Jantjes, 'Red Rags to a Bull', in *The Other Story* [essay in catalogue], Hayward Gallery, London 1989.
1990 Gavin Jantjes, *Print as a Specialism,* (Bradford, 1990), (text of a lecture given at the Eleventh British International Print Biennale conference in Bradford, 20 October 1990).
1988 Gavin Jantjes, *[Contemporary South African Art],* (Text of a lecture given at the African American Studies Association annual conference held in Chicago, October – November 1988).
1991 Gavin Jantjes, *Food for thought,* (Essay written for a conference on printmaking held at the Royal College of Art, London).
1991 *The Institute of International Visual Arts [InIVA]: Final report,* edited by Gavin Jantjes and Sarah Wason, (London: London Arts Board, 1991).
1993 Gavin Jantjes, 'The Artist as Cultural Salmon: A View from the Frying Pan', *Third Text,* no.23, (Summer 1993), 103-106.
1993 Gavin Jantjes, 'The Long March from the "Ethnic Arts" to "New Internationalism"', in *Cultural Diversity in the Arts, The Netherlands,* edited by Ria Lavrijsen, (Amsterdam: Royal Tropical Institute, 1993), pp.59-66.
1995 Gavin Jantjes, 'Who's listening?', in *To Be or Not To Be European: A Lousiana Debate on Modern Art and Culture, June 1994',* edited by Soren Molstrom, (Glydendal: The Eleni Nakou, Foundation, 1995), pp.35-41.
Reviews, articles, etc.:
– Pogus Caesar, *Korabra: Gavin Jantjes,* (Birmingham: Central TV, 1988). (video).
– 'Exhibitions: Gavin Jantjes Tribute to the School-Children of Soweto', *Sunday Times Magazine,* (8 January 1983), (Review of Gavin Jantjes show at the Midland Group Gallery, January – February 1983).
– John Furse, 'Gavin Jantjes' [Plymouth Arts Centre, England; exhibition], *Arts Review,* (24 April 1987), 274.
– Margaret Garlake, 'Gavin Jantjes' [Edward Totah Gallery, London; exhibition], *Art Monthly,* no.64, (March 1983), 18.
– Margaret Garlake, 'Gavin Jantjes at the Black Art Gallery', *Art Monthly,* no.87, (June 1985), 16.
– Mel Gooding, 'Gavin Jantjes: Westbourne Gallery', *Arts Review,* (12 October 1984), 502.
– 'Gavin Jantjes: Zulu', *Artrage,* no.26, (Autumn 1989), 35, (Stoke-on-Trent City Museum and Art Gallery).
– Julian Henriques, 'Image And Imagination: The Screenprints of Gavin Jantjes' [Black Art Gallery, London; exhibition], *Ten.8,* no.19, 50-51.
– Errol Lloyd, 'Gavin Jantjes' Recent Exhibition', *Artrage,* no.2, (February 1983), 4.
– *Signs of Resistance,* 1985: see Chronology.

Jarrett, Wendy
b.1964, Northampton, England.
Group exhibitions:
1988 *Black Art: Plotting the Course,* see Chronology.
Reviews, articles, texts, etc.:
Rita Keegan, 'Back to the Source', *Blackboard Review,* no.2, (1990), 40-42.

Jawahirilal, Lalitha
Dates Unavailable.
Group exhibition:
1985 *Mirror Reflecting Darkly,* see Chronology.
Reviews, articles, texts, etc.:
Amanda Sebestyen, 'Lallitha Jawahirilal', *City Limits,* (6 – 13 December 1990), 24.

Jegede, Emmanuel Taiwo
b.1943, Nigeria.
Solo exhibitions:
[n.d.] *Emmanuel Taiwo Jegede: The Joy Of A Living Race,* The October Gallery, London.
Group exhibitions:
1973 *Eight Commonwealth Artists,* see Chronology.
1985 *New Horizons,* see Chronology.
1986 *The Colours of Black,* see Chronology.
Reviews, articles, texts, etc.:
– Meshack Asare, *Emmanuel Taiwo Jegede: Paintings, Sculptures,*
  (Penzance: Alison Hodge, 1986).
– Alice Charles, 'Sculpturing a Vision from Africa', *The Weekly Journal,* (17 November 1994),12.
– Genevieve Fox, 'Emmanuel Jegede', [Royal Festival Hall, London; exhibition], *Arts Review,*
  (14 December 1990), 686.
– Margaret Garlake, 'Emmanuel Jegede', *Art Monthly,* no.96, (May 1986), 14,
  (Westbourne Gallery, London).
– Juwon, 'Jegede-Abibiman', *Home News,* (8 – 14 February 1990).
– David Lee, 'Emmanuel Jegede', [Westbourne Gallery, London; travelling exhibition],
  Arts Review, (31 January 1986), 42.

Johnson, Claudette
b.1959, Manchester, England.
Solo exhibitions:
1990 *Claudette Johnson: Pushing Back the Boundaries,*
  (Hebden Bridge: Urban Fox Press, 1990), (published on the occasion of an exhibition
  at Rochdale Art Gallery, 1990, curated by Lubaina Himid and text by Maud Sulter).
[n.d.] *Claudette Johnson: Portraits from a Small Room,* 198 Gallery, London.
Group exhibitions:
1982 *The Pan-Afrikan Connection: an Exhibition of Work by Young Black Artists – Good Ideals,*
  see Chronology.
1983 *The Pan-Afrikan Connection,* see Chronology.
1983 *5 Black Women,* see Chronology.
1984 *Into the Open: New Painting, Prints and Sculpture by Contemporary Black Artists,*
  see Chronology.

1985 *The Thin Black Line,* see Chronology.
1987 *The Image Employed,* see Chronology.
1993 *Reclaiming the Madonna: Artists as Mothers,* see Chronology.
Texts by Claudette Johnson:
1991 Claudette Johnson, 'Issues Surrounding the Representation of the Naked Body of a Woman', *FAN-Feminist Art News,* 3, no.8, 12-14.
1992 Claudette Johnson, 'Rethinking Radicalism', *FAN-Feminist Art News,* 4, no.1, 21.
Reviews, articles, etc.:
'Vision, Myth, Dream by Claudette Johnson', *Black Arts in London,* no.121, (1 – 28 February 1990), 10. (Tom Allen Centre, London).

Joseph, Tam
b.1947, Dominica.
Solo exhibitions:
1986 *Observers are Worried: Paintings and Sculpture by Tam Joseph,* introduction by Eddie Chambers, St. Pancras Library and Shaw Theatre Foyer, London.
1989 *Tam Joseph the Local Man,* One Spirit Gallery, London, (Press Release).
1989 *Tam Joseph: Learning to Walk,* Smith Art Gallery & Museum, Stirling, (Exhibition also shown at the Royal Festival Hall, London, December 1989 – February 1990).
Group exhibitions:
1984 *Into the Open: New Painting, Prints and Sculpture by Contemporary Black Artists,* see Chronology.
1985 *Black Skin/Bluecoat,* see Chronology.
1985 *GLC Anti-Racist Mural Project 1985,* see Chronology.
1986 *Double Vision,* see Chronology.
1986 *From Two Worlds,* see Chronology.
1987 *Comic Iconoclasm,* Institute of Contemporary Arts, London.
1987 *Critical Realism: Britain in the 1980's Through the Work of 28 Artists,* see Chronology.
1987 *The Image Employed: The Use of Narrative in Black Art,* see Chronology.
1988 *Black Art: Plotting the Course,* see Chronology.
1989 *The Artist Abroad,* see Chronology.
1991 *Shocks to the System: Social and Political Issues in Recent British Art from the Arts Council Collection,* see Chronology.
1993 *Black Artists and the British Flag,* see Chronology.
1994 *Us an' Dem,* see Chronology.
Texts by Tam Joseph:
[n.d.] Eddie Chambers and Tam Joseph, *The Artpack:* see General texts.
1988 Tam Joseph, 'Observers Are Worried', in *Storms of the Heart,* edited by Kwesi Owusu, (London: Camden Press, 1988), pp.31-38.
Reviews, articles, etc.:
_ Hiroko Hagiwara, 'Edgy Blues: Tam Joseph's Paintings Great White', *Third Text,* no.30, (Spring 1995), 89-93.
_ 'Tam Joseph – Apocalyptic Humour', *Artrage,* no.20, (1988), 32.
_ 'Tam Joseph: "Learning to Walk"', *Artrage,* no.26, (Autumn 1989), 35.
_ 'One Spirit Gallery', *Black Arts in London,* no.114, (1 – 31 May 1989), 13, (Preview of "Tam Joseph the Local Man").
_ Frank Ruhrmund, 'Tam Joseph' [Newlyn Orion Galleries, Penzance, England; exhibition], *Arts Review,* (26 February 1988), 126.
_ Ray Rushton, 'Tam Joseph' [The Minories, Colchester, England; travelling exhibition], *Arts Review,* (6 October 1989), 702.
_ *Signs Of Resistance,* 1985: see Chronology.

Julien, Isaac (see also Sankofa Film Collective)
b.1960, Place of Birth Unavailable.

Group exhibitions:
1984 *Into the Open,* see Chronology.
1987 *State of the Nation,* Herbert Gallery & Museum, Coventry.
1995 *Mirage,* see Chronology.

Texts by Isaac Julien:
1988 Isaac Julien and Kobena Mercer, 'Race, Sexual Politics and Masculinity: a Dossier',
in *Male Order: Unwrapping Masculinity,* edited by Rowena Chapman
and Jonathan Rutherford, (London: Lawrence & Wishart, 1988), pp.97-164.
1991 Amy Taubin, 'Soul to Soul' [interview], *Sight & Sound,* 1, (August 1991), 14-17.
1992 Isaac Julien, 'Black is, Black ain't' in *Black Popular Culture: a Project by Michelle Wallace,*
edited by Gina Dent, (Seattle: Bay Press, 1992), pp.255-263.
1992 Isaac Julien and Kobena Mercer, 'True Confessions: a Discourse on Images of Black Male
Sexuality,' *Ten.8,* no.22, 4-9, (reprinted in *Ten.8,* 2, no.3, (Spring 1992), 40-49.
[n.d.] Bruce Morrow, 'Interview with Isaac Julien', *Fuse,* 18, no.4, 15-23.

Reviews, articles, etc.:
_ Paul Burston, 'Shorts' (review), *Sight & Sound,* 3, (April 1993), 64-65.
_ Manthia Diawara, 'The Absent One: the Avant-Garde and the Black Imaginary
in "Looking for Langston"', *Wide Angle,* 13, no.3/4, (July – October 1991), 96-109.
_ Tony Fisher, 'Isaac Julien: "Looking for Langston Hughes" – Montage of a Dream Deferred',
Third Text, no.21, (Autumn 1990), 59-70, (includes an interview with Isaac Julien).
_ Paul Gilroy, 'Climbing the Racial Mountain: A Conversation with Isaac Julien', in *Small Acts:
Some Thoughts on the Politics of Black Cultures,* (London: Serpent's Tail, 1993), pp.166-172.
_ 'Isaac Julien: "Looking for Langston"', (performance, 1990), *Art & Design,*
(September – October 1994), 22.
_ Barbara Kruger, 'The Passion of Remembrance' (review), *Artforum,* (September 1988), 143.
_ Kobena Mercer, 'Dark & Lovely', *Ten.8,* 2, no.1, (1991), 78-85.
_ Cynthia Rose, 'A Walk on the Wild Side', *The Guardian,* (11 February 1994).
_ Adrian Searle 'Thumping Pleasure', *Artscribe,* no 89, (November – December 1991), 22-23.
_ Cherry Smyth, 'Queer Questions', *Sight & Sound,* 2, (September 1992), 34-35.
_ Greg Tate, 'The Cave: Greg Tate on "Looking for Langston"', *Artforum,* (December 1989),19-20.
_ 'Threatening Pleasures', (How the 1977 Jubilee, Music, Sexuality, Politics and Pleasure
Come Together in "Young Soul Rebels"; a discussion), Paul Gilroy, …et al., *Sight & Sound,* 1,
(August 1991), 7-19.

Kapoor, Anish
b.1954, Bombay, India.

Solo exhibitons:
1983 *Anish Kapoor: Feeling into Form,* Walker Art Gallery, Liverpool.
1983 *Anish Kapoor,* Galerie 't Venster, Rotterdam.
1983 *Anish Kapoor,* Kunsthalle, Basel.
1986 *Anish Kapoor,* Kunstnernes Hus, Oslo.
1986 *Anish Kapoor: Recent Sculpture and Drawings,* University Gallery,
University of Massachusetts, Amherst.
1986 *Sensual Transcendence: the Sculpture of Anish Kapoor,* Albright-Knox Art Gallery, Buffalo.
1990 *Anish Kapoor,* British Pavilion, Venice Biennale.
1991 *Anish Kapoor: Drawings,* Tate Gallery, London.
1993 *Anish Kapoor: White Sand, Red Millet, Many Flowers,* South Bank Centre, London.

Group exhibitions:
1981 *British Sculpture in the 20th Century,* Whitechapel Art Gallery, London.
1981 *Objects And Sculpture,* Institute of Contemporary Arts, London.
1982 *Englische Plastik Heute = English Sculpture Now,* Kunstmuseum, Lucerne.
1983 *New Art,* Tate Gallery, London.
1983 *The Sculpture Show: Fifty Sculptors at the Serpentine and the South Bank,* Hayward Gallery, Serpentine Gallery, London.
1983 *Transformations: New Sculpture from Britain,* Sao Paulo Bienal: British Pavilion.
1984 *The British Art Show: Old Allegiances and New Directions, 1979 – 1984,* Arts Council of Great Britain, London.
1984 *An International Survey of Recent Painting and Sculpture,* Museum of Modern Art, New York.
1985 *The British Show,* Art Gallery of New South Wales, Sydney.
1985 *The Poetic Object,* Douglas Hyde Gallery, Dublin.
1987 *A Quiet Revolution: British Sculpture Since 1965,* Museum of Contemporary Art, Chicago and Museum of Modern Art, San Francisco.
1987 *Viewpoint: British Art in the 1980s,* Museum of Modern Art, Brussels.
1988 *Starlit Waters: British Sculpture – an International Art 1968 – 1988,* Tate Gallery, Liverpool, (texts by Martin Kunz, Charles Harrison and Lynne Cooke).
1990 *Affinities and Intuitions: The Gerald S. Elliott Collection of Contemporary Art,* published on the occasion of an exhibition held at the Art Institute of Chicago, (London: Thames & Hudson, 1990).
1991 *The Turner Prize: An Exhibition of Work by Ian Davenport, Anish Kapoor, Fiona Rae and Rachel Whiteread,* Tate Gallery, London.
1992 *New Voices: New Works for the British Council Collection,* British Council, London.
1994 *Sculptors' Drawings: Presented by the Weltkunst Foundation,* Tate Gallery, London.
1995 *Contemporary British Art in Print: The Publications of Charles Booth Clibborn and his Imprint the Paragon Press, 1986 – 1995.* Scottish National Gallery of Art, Edinburgh.
Reviews, articles, texts, etc.: (for fuller listing see Art Index)
 _ Richard Dorment, 'Vexed Question of Colour', *Weekend Telegraph,* (9 December 1989), (review of Lisson Gallery show).
 _ Andrew Graham-Dixon, 'Pride & Prejudice', *The Independent,* (5 December 1989), (review of Lisson Gallery show).
 _ 'Anish Kapoor: Venice Biennale 1990', [interviewed by William Furlong], in *Audio Arts: Discourse And Practice In Contemporary Art,* (London, 1994).
 _ Corneil Van der Speck, 'Anish Kapoor' [The Power Plant, Toronto: exhibition], *C Magazine,* no.41, (Spring 1994), 48-49.

Karimjee, Mumtaz
b.1950, Bombay, India.
Group exhibitions:
1986 *Darshan,* see Chronology.
1986 *Jagrati,* see Chronology.
1986 *Reflections of the Black Experience,* see Chronology.
1987 *Polareyes,* see Chronology.
1989 *Fabled Territories,* see Chronology.
1990 *Autoportraits,* see Chronology.
1990 *In Focus,* Horizon Gallery, London.
1992 *Fine Material for a Dream…?: A Reappraisal of Orientalism,* see Chronology.
Reviews, articles, texts, etc.:
 _ Manick Govinda, 'Against the Clause Exhibition', *Bazaar,* no.5, (Summer 1988), 20-21.
 _ Sunil Gupta, 'Photography, Sexuality & Cultural Difference: the Emergence of Black Lesbian

and Gay Identities in the UK', "Disputed Indentities", *SF Camerawork Quarterly,* 17, no.3, (Fall 1990), 19-26.
_ 'In Focus', *Black Arts in London,* no.122, (1 – 31 March 1990), 9.
_ 'Mis[sed] Representations: Recent Work by David Lewis and Mumtaz Karimjee', *Ten.8: Critical Decade,* 2, no.3, (Spring 1992), 146-147.
_ 'Mumtaz Karimjee', *Polareyes,* no.1, (1987), [26-28].
_ Mumtaz Karimjee and Amina Patel, 'Aurat Shakti', *Ten.8: Critical Decade,* 2, no.3, (Spring 1992), 62-63.
_ 'My Mother, My Sisters, Myself', *Artrage,* no.22/23 (Winter 1988), 16-17, (Exhibition at Sisterwrite Bookshop, London, 1988).
_ 'Two Recent Exhibitions by Asian Women', *FAN-Feminist Art News,* 2, no.9, (1989), 15.

Kaur, Perminder
b.1965, Nottingham, England.
Group exhibitions:
1990 *"Let the Canvas Come to Life with Dark Faces",* see Chronology.
1991 *Four x 4,* see Chronology.
1992 *BBC Billboard Project,* see Chronology.
1992 *BT New Contemporaries 1992,* Newlyn Orion, Penzance, and other venues.
1995 *The British Art Show 4,* see Chronology.
Reviews, articles, texts, etc.:
Emma Anderson, 'Four from Four x 4', *Women's Art Magazine,* no.44, (January – February 1992), 12-13.

Keegan, Rita
b.1949, New York, USA.
Group exhibitions:
1983 *Women's Work I,* Brixton Art Gallery, London.
1985 *Brixton Artists Collective Ltd,* Brixton Art Gallery, London.
1985 *Mirror Reflecting Darkly,* see Chronology.
1985 *Women's Work V Shows Love, Sex, & Romance,* Brixton Art Gallery, London.
1986 *Brixton Artists Collective Ltd, 50 Not Out,* Brixton Art Gallery, London.
1986 *Black Women in View,* see Chronology.
1986 *Tangled Roots: Mixed Media Exhibition,* see Chronology.
1990 *"Let the Canvas Come to Life with Dark Faces,"* see Chronology.
1991 *Four x 4,* see Chronology.
1992 *Trophies of Empire,* see Chronology.
1992 *White Noise,* see Chronology.
1994 *Time Machine: Ancient Eygpt and Contemporary Art,* British Museum, London, in asociation with inIVA.
1994 *With Your Own Face on,* see Chronology.
Reviews, articles, texts, etc.:
_ *Issues in Women's Studies: Outside in – Women Artists and Cultural Difference,* Programme 7, Open University, Milton Keynes, 1991. (video).
_ Rita Keegan, 'Back to the Source: Rita Keegan Assesses the Changing State of the Art of Crafts', *Blackboard Review,* no.2, (1990), 40-42.
_ Clare Rendell, 'Actual Lives of Women Artists: Rita Keegan 1987' [interview], *Women Artists Slide Library Journal,* (October – November 1987), 10-11.

Kelly, George (Onar-F'owokan),
b.1943, Kingston, Jamaica.
Solo exhibitions:
1994 *Beyond My Grandfather's Dreams: An Exhibition of Sculpture by Fowokan,*
Jamaica High Commission, London, (foreword by Stuart Hall).
Group exhibitions:
1983 *Heart in Exile,* see Chronology.
1985 *3rd Creation for Liberation,* see Chronology.
1985 *From Generation to Generation, (The installation),* see Chronology.
1985 *New Horizons,* see Chronology.
1986 *The Colours of Black,* see Chronology.
1988 *Contemporary Art by Afro-Caribbean Artists,* see Chronology.
1986 *The Colours of Black,* see Chronology.
1987 *OBAALA's Marcus Garvey Centenary Show,* see Chronology.
1987 *Creation for Liberation Open Exhibition,* see Chronology.
Reviews, articles, texts, etc.:
'Recent Work', [198 Gallery], *Black Arts In London,* no.123, (1 – 30 April 1990), 10.

Kempadoo, Roshini
b.1959, Sussex, England.
Group exhibitions:
1990 *Autoportraits,* see Chronology.
1990 *Disputed Identities,* see Chronology.
1991 *Black Markets,* see Chronology.
1991 *Interrogating Identity,* see Chronology.
1992 *Confrontations,* see Chronology.
1992 *Who Do You Take Me For?,* see Chronology.
Reviews, articles, texts, etc.:
_ Helen Cadwallader, 'The Big Issue: Shifting Borders in Newcastle',
[Laing Gallery, Newcastle: exhibition], *Creative Camera,* no.20, (February, March 1993), 49.
_ Kellie Jones, 'In their own Image', (Black Women Artists who Combine Text with
Photography), *Artforum,* (November 1990), 132-138.
_ 'Section Three: Portfolio – Roshini Kempadoo', in *Passion,* edited by Maud Sulter,
(Hebden Bridge: Urban Fox Press, 1990), pp.208-210.

Khan, Keith
Dates Unavailable.
Group exhibitions:
1991 *Jashan-E-Bahar,* see Chronology.
1993 *Captives,* see Chronology.
1995 *Mirage,* see Chronology.
Reviews, articles, texts, etc.:
_ Manick Govinda, 'Against the Clause Exhibition', *Bazaar,* no.5, (Summer 1988), 20-21.
_ Devdan Sen, 'Keith Khan', *Bazaar,* no.7, (1989), [2-5].

Khanna, Balraj
b.1940, Punjab, India.
Solo exhibitions:
1987 *Balraj Khanna,* Horizon Gallery, London.

Group exhibitions:
1981 *Tapisseries de la Manufacture de Portalegre,* Musee d'art moderne de la Ville de Paris, Paris.
1989 *The Other Story,* see Chronology.
1989 *The Tree of Life,* South Bank Centre, London.
Texts by Balraj Khanna:
1986 Balraj Khanna, Richard Cork and Shirley Read, *Art on the South Bank: An Independent Report,* (London: Greater London Council, 1986).
1989 Balraj Khanna, 'England: my Brave New World' [catalogue essay], in *The Other Story,* Hayward Gallery, London.
1993 *Kalighat: Indian Popular Painting 1800 – 1930,* South Bank Centre, London.
Reviews, articles, etc.:
  _ Allan de Souza, 'Balraj Khanna: the Artist Who Came in from the Cold', *Bazaar,* no.18, (Autumn 1991), 21.
  _ Peter Dormer, 'Balraj Khanna' [October Gallery, London; exhibition], *Art Monthly,* no.38, (1980), 34-35.
  _ Mel Gooding, 'Balraj Khanna' [Air Gallery, London; exhibition], *Art Monthly,* no.73, (February 1984), 23-24.
  _ Mel Gooding, 'Balraj Khanna: Air Gallery', *Arts Review,* (17 February 1984), 72-73.
  _ Elizabeth Hilliard, 'Balraj Khanna' [Horizon Gallery, London; exhibition], *Arts Review,* 39, (8 May 1987), 296.
  _ 'Balraj Khanna', [South Bank Centre, London; exhibition], *Black Arts in London,* no.123 (1 – 30 April 1990), 9.
  _ Rakesh Mathur, 'Balraj Khanna', *Artrage,* no.22/23, (Winter 1988), 10.

Lamba, Jaginder
b.1948, Kenya.
Solo exhibitions:
1985 *Juginder Lamba: Relics,* Rochdale Art Gallery, Rochdale.
1988 *Juginder Lamba: an Exhibition of Sculptures,* Horizon Gallery, London, (card).
1995 *Juginder Lamba: From the Wood, an Exhibition by the John Moores University Sculpture Fellow, 1994 – 1995, Funded by the Henry Moore Foundation,* Bluecoat Gallery, Liverpool.
Group exhibitons:
1984 *Into the Open: New Painting, Prints and Sculpture by Contemporary Black Artists,* see Chronology.
1985 *Combinations: Lubaina Himid/Jaginder Lamba,* see Chronology.
1989 *One Spirit: Black Artists against Racism,* see Chronology.
1992 *Trophies of Empire,* see Chronology.
Texts by Juginder Lamba:
1988 *The Art Pack: A History of Black Artists in Britain,* (London: Haringey Arts Council, 1988), (texts by Eddie Chambers and Juginder Lamba).
Reviews, articles, etc.:
  _ Sabita Banerji, 'Juginder Lamba "…Awaiting its Second Metamorphosis,"' *Artrage,* no.13, (1986), 28.
  _ Andrew Hughes, 'Juginder Lamba' [Horizon Gallery, London], *Arts Review,* (7 October 1988), 695.
  _ David Lee, 'Juginder Lamba' [Commonwealth Institute, London], *Arts Review,* (28 March 1986), 168.

Lamba, Manjeet
b.1953, Nairobi, Kenya.
Group exhibitions:
1990 *"Let the Canvas Come to Life with Dark Faces"*, see Chronology.
1992 *Crossing Black Waters*, see Chronology.
1993 *Black People and the British Flag*, see Chronology.

Landell, Trevor
b.1961, England.
Group exhibitions:
1985 *3rd Creation for Liberation*, see Chronology.
1987 *Creation for Liberation Open Exhibition*, see Chronology.
Reviews, articles, texts, etc.:
'Trevor Landel', *Artrage*, (Summer 1991), 30, (181 Gallery, London).

Lawar, Roland
b.1949, Nigeria.
Group exhibitions:
1985 *3rd Creation for Liberation*, see Chronology.
1990 *"Let the Canvas Come to Life with Dark Faces"*, see Chronology.

Lee, Godfrey
Jamaica, Dates Unavailable.
Group exhibitions:
1988 *Black Art: Plottting the Course*, see Chronology.
1990 *"Let the Canvas Come to Life with Dark Faces"*, see Chronology.
1991 *History and Identity: Seven Painters*, see Chronology.

Lee, Rosa
b.1957, Place of Birth Unavailable.
Solo exhibitions:
1989 *Rosa Lee: Ellipsis*, Winchester Gallery, Winchester School of Art.
1990 *Rosa Lee*, Todd Gallery, London.
1992 *Rosa Lee*, Todd Gallery, London.
Group exhibitions:
1986 *The Class of '86: ILEA London Institute Show*, Royal Festival Hall, London.
1989 *John Moores Liverpool Exhibition 16*, Walker Art Gallery, Liverpool.
1992 *(dis)parities*, Mappin Art Gallery, Sheffield.
Texts by Rosa Lee:
1989 Rebecca Fortnum and Gill Houghton, 'Six Interviews 12.88…Rosa Lee', *Women Artists Slide Library Journal*, no.28, (April – May 1989), 8-9.
1987 Rosa Lee, 'Resisting Amnesia: Feminism, Painting and Postmodernism, *Feminist Review*, no.26, (Summer 1987), 5-28.
Reviews, articles, etc.:
– Tony Godfrey, 'A British Painting for the '90s', *Art in America*, (April 1991), 144-153.
– Sarah Kent, 'Rosa Lee: Todd Gallery', *Time Out*, (29 March – 5 April 1995), 51.
– Angela McRobbie, 'Women and the Arts into the 1990s', *Alba*, (May 1991), 4-12.
– Margaret Walters, 'Rosa Lee: Painting as Lace-Making', *Modern Painters*, (Spring 1992), 71-72.

Lewis, David
b.1962, Place of Birth Unavailable.
Group exhibitions:
1986 *Reflections of the Black Experience,* see Chronology.
1987 *D-Max,* see Chronology.
1995 *The Impossible Science of Being,* see Chronology.
Reviews, articles, texts, etc.:
– 'Mis[sed] Representations: Recent work by David Lewis and Mumtaz Karimjee',
  Ten.8: Critical Decade, 2, no.3, (Spring 1992), 146-147.
– Gilane Tawadros, 'Other Britains, other Britons', *Aperture,* no.113, (Winter 1988), 40-46.
– Gilane Tawadros, 'Redrawing the Boundaries: the Documentary Work of David Lewis
  and Maxine Walker', *Ten.8, Critical Decade,* 2, no.3, (Spring 1992), 86-92.

Lewis, Susan
Dates Unavailable.
Reviews, articles, texts, etc.:
'Artists Pages', in *Let's Get it on: The Politics of Black Performance,*
edited by Catherine Ugwu, (London: Institute of Contemporary Arts, 1995), pp.144-149.

Lloyd, Errol
b.1943, Jamaica.
Group exhibitions:
1971 *Caribbean Artists in England,* see Chronology.
1985 *3rd Creation for Liberation,* see Chronology.
1986 *Caribbean Expressions in Britain,* see Chronology.
1988 *Black Art: Plotting the Course,* see Chronology.
Reviews, articles, texts, etc.:
Fay Rodrigues, 'Errol Lloyd Leaves MAAS: an Appreciation', *Artrage,* no.12, (Spring 1986), 17.

Locke, Donald
b.1930, Stewartville, Guyana.
Group exhibitions:
1971 *Caribbean Artists in England,* see Chronology.
1978 *Afro-Caribbean Art,* see Chronology.
1989 *The Other Story,* see Chronology.
Reviews, articles, texts, etc.:
'Donald Locke, Phoenix (Ariz.) ARTSPACE', *South Western Contemporary Arts Quarterly,* [n.d.].

Lyons, John
b.1933, Port of Spain, Trinidad.
Solo exhibitions:
1992 *John Lyons: 'Behind the Carnival', Myths and Legends,* Huddersfield Art Gallery.
Group exhibitions:
1986 *Caribbean Expressions in Britain,* see Chronology.
1988 *Black Art: Plotting the Course,* see Chronology.
1988 *Revelations of Black,* see Chronology.
1990 *"Let the Canvas Come to Life with Dark Faces",* see Chronology.
1995 *The Caribbean Connection,* see Chronology.

McCalla, Kenneth
b.1961, England.
Group exhibitions:
1985 *3rd Creation for Liberation,* see Chronology.
1985 *From Generation to Generation, (The Installation),* see Chronology.
1987 *Creation for Liberation Open Exhibition,* see Chronology.
1987 *OBAALA's Marcus Garvey Centenary Show,* see Chronology.

McKenzie, Jenny
Dates Unavailable.
Group exhibitions:
1987 *Polareyes,* see Chronology.
1989 *One Spirit: Black Artists Against Racism,* see Chronology.
Reviews, articles, texts, etc.:
Jenny McKenzie, 'Visual Perceptions of a Two Year Old', *Polareyes,* no.1, (1987), 5-7.

McQueen, Steve
b.1969, London, England.
Group exhibitions:
1994 *Acting Out: The Body In Video, Then And Now,* Royal College of Art, London.
1995 *The British Art Show 4,* see Chronology.
1995 *Mirage,* see Chronology.
1996 *Spellbound,* Hayward Gallery, London.

Malik, Naiza
b.1968 Bahawalphur, Pakistan.
Group exhibitions:
1988 *Numaish Lalit Kala,* see Chronology.
1990 *In Focus,* see Chronology.

Mathison, Trevor (see also Black Audio Film Collective)
b.1960, London, England.
Group exhibitions:
1987 *The Image of Employed: The Use of Narrative in Black Art,* see Chronology.
1995 *Mirage,* see Chronology.

Medalla, David
b.1942, Manila, Phillipines.
Group exhibitions:
1989 *The Other Story,* see Chronology.
1991 *Shocks to the System: Social and Political Issues in Recent British Art from the Arts Council Collection,* see Chronology.
Texts by David Medalla:
1964 *Signals,* edited by David Medalla, London, 1964 – 1966, [Periodical].
1977 'David Medalla in Conversation with Brandon Taylor', *Artscribe,* no.6, (April 1977), 20-23.
1977 David Medalla, *Tatlin at the Funeral Of Malevitch: a Performance Art Work,* (London, 1977).
1988 David Medalla, 'Memories of the Sixties: Paris – London',

And-Journal of Art and Art Education, no.17, 8-17.
1989 David Medalla, 'Signals' [catalogue essay], in *The Other Story,* Hayward Gallery, London.
1996 *Signals: Box Set,* (London: InIVA, 1996).
Reviews, articles, etc.:
– Rasheed Araeen, 'Conversation with David Medalla', *Black Phoenix,* no.3, (Spring 1979),10-19.
– Guy Brett, 'Both Author and Reader', *C Magazine,* no.36, (Winter 1993), 18-28.
– Guy Brett, 'Le Cinetisme et la Tradition en Peinture et Sculpture', *Artstudio,* no.22, (Automme 1991), 84-93.
– Guy Brett, 'David Medalla: A Certain Way of Life', *Art & Design,* [Art & Cultural Difference: Hybrids and Clusters], 10, no.7/8, (July – August 1995), 66-75.
– Guy Brett, 'David Medalla: from Biokinetecism to Synoptic Realism', *Third Text,* no.8/9, (Autumn – Winter 1989), 79-112.
– Guy Brett, *Exploding Galaxies: The Art of David Medalla,* (London: Kala Press, 1995).
– Guy Brett, 'Impromptus: David Medalla', *Art in America,* (November 1989), 156-163.
– Guy Brett, 'Terre et musee-local ou global?', *Cahiers du Musee National d'Art Moderne,* no.28, (Summer 1989), 93-102.
– Richard Dyer, 'David Medalla', *Frieze,* no.21, (March – April 1995), 66-67.
– Mel Gooding, 'David Medalla', *Art Monthly,* no.184, (March 1995), 34-36.
– Alistair Mackintosh, 'Art For Whom?' [interview], *Art & Artists,* (January 1973) 26-31.
– Jun Terra, 'David Medalla in London', *Third Text,* no.30, (Spring 1995), 93-100.

Merali, Shaheen
b.1959, Tanzania.
Solo exhibitions:
1989 *The Fire or the Garden by Shaheen Merali,* Tom Allen Centre, London.
Group exhibitions:
1985 *New Horizons,* see Chronology.
1986 *The Colours of Black,* see Chronology.
1987 *Creation for Liberation Open Exhibition,* see Chronology.
1988 *Contemporary Art by Afro-Caribbean Artists,* see Chronology.
1989 *The Artist Abroad,* see Chronology.
1989 *Fabled Territories,* see Chronology.
1989 *One Spirit: Black Artists Against Racism,* see Chronology.
1990 *"Distinguishing Marks",* see Chronology.
1991 *Four x 4,* see Chronology.
1992 *Confrontations,* see Chronology.
1992 *Crossing Black Waters,* see Chronology.
1992 *Trophies of Empire,* see Chronology.
1993 *Beyond Destination,* see Chronology.
1995 *Fotofeis: International Festival of Photography in Scotland,* Edinburgh, Fotofeis, (Shaheen Merali: "Paradigm Lost", a Scottish Arts Council touring exhibition), pp.92-93.
Reviews, articles, texts, etc.:
– Emmanuel Cooper, 'On Black Art', *Time Out,* (6 February 1989), 39.
– 'Fire or the Garden', *Black Arts in London,* no.111, (1 February – 1 March 1989), 12
– Andrew Hope, 'In Search of Roots: Shaheen Merali Art Exhibition', *Race Today Review,* (1988), 40-41
– 'Recent Work [198 Gallery]', *Black Arts in London,* no.123 (1 – 30 April 1990), 10
– Amanda Sebestyen, 'Different Diasporas', *New Statesman & Society,* (3 February 1989), 49.

Ming, Bill
b.1944, Bermuda.
Solo exhibitions:
1993 *Bill Ming: Two Rock Passage to Liverpool: An Exhibition by the First Holder of Liverpool John Moores Univesity Fellowship in Sculpture, Funded by The Henry Moore Foundation,* Bluecoat Gallery, Liverpool.
Group exhibitions:
1984 *Into the Open: New Painting, Prints and Sculpture by Contemporary Black Artists,* see Chronology.
1986 *Caribbean Expressions in Britain,* see Chronology.
1995 *The Caribbean Connection,* see Chronology.
Reviews, articles, texts, etc.:
Tessa Sidey, 'Bill Ming' [Birmingham Museums and Art Gallery, England; exhibition], *Arts Review,* (11 September 1987), 613.

Mistry, Dhruva
b.1957, Kanjari, India.
Solo exhibitions:
1985 *Dhruva Mistry: Sculpture and Drawings,* Kettle's Yard Gallery, Cambridge.
1987 *Dhruva Mistry,* Artsite Gallery, Bath.
1990 *Dhruva Mistry: Bronzes 1985 – 1990,* Nigel Greenwood Gallery, London.
Group exhibitions:
1988 *Graven Images: Art, Religion and Politics,* see Chronology.
1993 *Recent British Sculpture from the Arts Council Collection,* see Chronology.
Reviews, articles, texts, etc.:
_ Nick Axarlis, 'Indian Sculptures at the V & A', *Artrage,* no.20, (Summer 1988), 26.
_ Mary Rose Beaumont, 'Dhruva Mistry', [Nigel Greenwood Gallery, London; exhibition], *Arts Review,* (23 October 1987), 719-720.
_ David Cohen, 'Out of India: Hindu Spirituality in Recent British Sculpture', *Sculpture,* 13, (January – February 1994), 20-27.
_ Nena Dimitrijevic, 'Hayward Annual', *Flash Art,* no.123, (Summer 1985), 58.
_ 'Dhruva Mistry, "Guardian 2"', *Arts Magazine,* (October 1985), 139.
_ William Feaver, 'Dhruva Mistry' [Nigel Greenwood Gallery, London; exhibition], *Art News,* (January 1988), 183.
_ William Feaver, 'Dhruva Mistry', [Nigel Greenwood Gallery, London; exhibition], *Art News,* (February 1991), 158.
_ Charles Harrison and Judy Annear, 'The Hayward Annual', *Art Monthly,* no.87, (June 1985), 3-6.
_ David Lillington, 'Dhruva Mistry', [Nigel Greenwood Gallery, London; exhibition], *Arts Review,* (2 November 1990), 597.
_ 'Man and Beast', [by CC], *Studio International,* no.1009, 198, (December 1985), 40-41.
_ Rupert Martin, 'Dhruva Mistry' [Nigel Greenwood Gallery, London; exhibition], *Flash Art,* no.138, (January – February 1988), 129.
_ Beatrice Phillpotts, 'Works in Clay' (Nigel Greenwood Gallery, London), *Arts Review,* (17 January 1986), 12.
_ Nadir Tharani, 'Dhruva Mistry: Royal Artefacts', *Bazaar,* no.18 (Autumn 1991), 7-8.

Mitchell, Sherlee
Dates Unavailable.
Reviews, articles, texts, etc.:
'Section Three: Portfolio – Sherlee Mitchell', in *Passion,* edited by Maud Sulter,
(Hebden Bridge: Urban Fox Press, 1990), pp.196-197.

Mitha, Alnoor
b.1961, Uganda, East Africa.
Group exhibitions:
1987 *Revelations of Black,* see Chronology.
1988 *Numaish Lalit Kala,* see Chronology.
1990 *In Focus,* see Chronology.

Mohanti, Prafulla
Dates Unavailable.
Group exhibitions:
1990 *In Focus,* see Chronology.
Texts by Prafulla Mohanti:
1988 Prafulla Mohanti, 'Art as Life', *Artrage,* no.20, 9-13.
1990 Prafulla Mohanti, 'East West Encounter', *Art Monthly,* no.132,
(December 1989 – January 1990), 13-14, 16-17.
Reviews, articles, etc.:
_ Allan de Souza, 'Prafulla Mohanti', *Bazaar,* no.9, 18-19, (Horizon Gallery, London,
August – September, 1989).
_ Sunil Gupta, 'Prafulla Mohanti: Under the Banyan Tree', *Bazaar,* no.18 (Autumn 1991), 22.
_ 'South Bank Centre', *Black Arts in London,* no.124, (1 – 30 June 1990), 10.

Moo-Young, Tony
b.1954, Port Antonio, Jamaica.
Group exhibitions:
1984 *Into the Open: New Painting, Prints and Sculpture by Contemporary Black Artists,*
see Chronology.
1988 *Contemporary Art by Afro-Caribbean Artists,* see Chronology.

Moody, Ronald
b.1900, Jamaica; died 1984, London, England.
Group exhibitions:
1971 *Caribbean Artists in England,* see Chronology.
1986 *Caribbean Expressions in Britain,* see Chronology.
1989 *The Other Story,* see Chronology.
1995 *The Caribbean Connection,* see Chronology.
Reviews, articles, texts, etc.:
_ Cynthia Moody, 'Ronald Moody: A Man True to his Vision, *Third Text,* no.8/9
(Autumn – Winter 1989), 5-24.
_ 'Ronald Moody: Obituary', *The Times,* (25 February 1984), 10.

Niati, Houria
b.1948, Algeria.
Solo exhibitions:
1988 *An Exhibition of Pastels & Paintings by Houria Niati,* Africa Centre, London.
Group exhibitions:
1983 *5 Black Women,* see Chronology.
1984 *Into the Open: New Painting, Prints and Sculpture by Contemporary Black Artists,*
see Chronology.
1986 *From Two Worlds,* see Chronology.
1991 *Four x 4,* see Chronology.
Reviews, articles, texts, etc.:
_ Emma Anderson, 'Four from Four x 4', *Women's Art Magazine,* no.44,
(January – February 1992), 12-13.
_ Sue Hubbard, 'Houria Niati', *Time Out,* (12 – 19 December 1990), 31,
(Rochan Gallery, London).
_ 'Interview with Houria Niati', *Gen,* (Spring 1984), 27-33, [reprinted from *Spare Rib,* April 1984].
_ Susan Morris, 'Forms of Intuition', *Arts Review,* (5 May 1989), 356.
_ 'Osmosis: Houria Niati', *Black Arts in London,* no.123 (1 – 30 April 1990), 9,
(Small Mansion Arts Centre, London).
_ Kwesi Owusu, 'Profile of Houria Niati', *Artrage,* no.6 (Spring 1984), 6-7.
_ Nigel Pollitt, 'Houria Niati', *City Limits,* (27 January – 2 February 1983),
(Review of "Delerium" at the Africa Centre, London).
_ Maud Sulter, 'Houria Niati, Black Woman Time Now',
in *Framing Feminism: Art and the Women's Movement, 1970 – 1985,*
edited by Griselda Pollock and Rozsika Parker, (London: Pandora, 1987), pp.259

Nichols, Colin
b.1952, Place of Birth Unavailable.
Group exhibitions:
1986 *Caribbean Expressions in Britain,* see Chronology.
1990 *"Let the Canvas Come to Life with Dark Faces",* See Chronology.

Nimarkoh, Virginia
b. 1967, London, England.
Group exhibitions:
1991 *Four x 4,* see Chronology.
1994 *Mise en Scène,* Institute of Contemporary Arts, London.
1995 *Care and Control,* see Chronology.
Texts by Virginia Nimarkoh:
1993 *The Phone Box: Art in Telephone Boxes,* (London: Virginia Nimarkoh/Bookworks, 1993),
(edition of 300 with original artists works).
1993 Virginia Nimarkoh, *Postcard,* [Artists book consisting of 144 colour postcards forming one
composite image], (London: Book Works, 1993).
Reviews, articles, etc.:
_ Emma Anderson, 'Four from Four x 4', *Women's Art Magazine,* no.44,
(January – February 1992), 12-13.
_ Katy Deepwell, 'Uncanny Resemblances: the Restaging of the mise en scène',
Women's Art Magazine, no.62, (January – February 1995), 17-19.
_ Jaki Irvine, 'Mise en Scène', *Third Text,* no.30 (Spring 1995), 101-106.

Nsusha, Benjamin Nhlanhla
b.1942, Port Shepstone District, South Africa.
Group exhibitions:
1984 *Into the Open: New Painting, Prints and Sculpture by Contemporary Black Artists,* see Chronology.
1985 *New Horizons,* see Chronology.
Texts by Benjamin Nsusha:
1988 Benjamin Nhlanhla Nsusha, *Black Artists within the Apartheid System,* Chelsea School of Art, BA Thesis.
Reviews, articles, etc.:
Dave Lee, 'Ben Nsusha, Marc Boothe', *Arts Review,* (11 May 1984), 235.

Ntuli, Pitika
b.1952, South Africa.
Group exhibitions:
1983 *Heart in Exile,* see Chronology.
1984 *Into the Open: New Painting, Prints and Sculpture by Contemporary Black Artists,* see Chronology.
1985 *3rd Creation for Liberation,* see Chronology.
1990 *"Distinguishing marks",* see Chronology.
Texts by Pitika Ntuli:
1986 Pitika Ntuli, 'In my Country', *Artrage,* no.14, 13.
1988 Pitika Ntuli, 'Orature: a Self-portrait', in *Storms of the Heart,* edited by Kwesi Owusu, (London: Camden Press, 1988), pp.209-218.
Reviews, articles, etc.:
_ '198 Gallery "Inkaba: Open Veins": the Backbone of Our Struggle', *Black Arts in London,* no.117, (1 – 30 September 1989), 11.
_ 'At the Nerve End of Our Dream', *Black Arts In London,* no.124, (1 – 30 June 1990), 8, (Greenwich Citizens Gallery, London).
_ 'Pitika Ntuli: Inkaba', *Artrage,* no.26, (Autumn 1989), 35, (198 Gallery, London).

Odonkor, Mowbray
b.1962, London, England.
Group exhibitions:
1985 *3rd Creation for Liberation,* see Chronology.
1987 *Creation for Liberation Open Exhibition,* see Chronology.
1987 *The Image Employed: The Use of Narrative in Black Art,* see Chronology.
1988 *Black Art: Plotting The Course,* see Chronology.
1988 *Incantations: Reclaiming Imagination,* see Chronology.
1991 *History and Identity: Seven Painters,* see Chronology.
1993 *Black People and the British Flag,* see Chronology.
Reviews, articles, texts, etc.:
Charles Hall, 'History & Identity', (Commonwealth Institute, London), *Arts Review,* (March 1992), 90.

Ofili, Chris
b.1968, Manchester, England.
Group exhibitions:
1993 *Borderless Print,* see Chronology.

1993 *RCA 1993: Painting School Degree Show,* Royal College of Art, London.
1995 *Brilliant! New Art from London,* Walker Art Center, Minneapolis.
1995 *The British Art Show 4,* see Chronology.
1995 *19th John Moores Liverpool exhibition, 1995 – 1996,* Walker Art Gallery, Liverpool.
Reviews, articles, texts, etc.:
 – Tania Guha, 'Cocaine Orgasm' [Bankspace, London: exhibition], *Time Out,* (13 – 21 December 1995), 56.
 – Stuart Morgan, 'The Elephant Man (for Dave Hickey): Stuart Morgan on Chris Ofili', *Frieze,* no.15, (March – April 1994), 40-43.

Oguibe, Olu
b.1964, Nigeria.
Solo exhibitions:
 1991 *Olu Oguibe: Works and Words,* Bhownagree Gallery, Commonwealth Institute, London.
Group exhibitions:
 1994 *Seen|Unseen,* see Chronology.
Texts by Olu Oguibe:
 1993 Olu Oguibe [guest editor] 'Africa', *Third Text,* Special Issue, no.23, (Summer 1993).
 1993 Olu Oguibe, 'In the Heart of Darkness', *Third Text,* Special Issue, no.23, (Summer 1993), 3-8.
 1994 Olu Oguibe, 'A Brief Note on Internationalism', in *Global Visions,* edited by Jean Fisher, (London: inIVA, 1994), pp.50-59.
 1994 Olu Oguibe, 'Beyond Gobineau', *Third Text,* no.25, (Winter 1993 – 1994), 105-111.
 1995 Olu Oguibe, *Uzo Egonu: An African Artist in the West,* (London: Kala Press, 1995).
Reviews, articles, etc.:
 – 'Censored!', *Artrage,* (Summer 1991), 31.
 – 'Commonwealth Institute', *Black Arts in London,* no.134, (1 – 31 March 1991), 6.
 – Okwui Enwezor, 'Occupied Territories: Power, Access and African Art' [africa95], *Frieze,* no.26, (January – February 1996), 37-41.
 – Anthony Ilona, 'Olu Oguibe: Recent Works', *Third Text,* no.25, (Winter 1993 – 94), 87-89.
 – Henry Lydiate and James Odling-Smee, 'Artlaw: F**K', *Art Monthly,* no.146, (May 1991), 33-34, (Commonwealth Institute, London).

Olubo, Joseph
Dates Unavailable.
Group exhibitions:
 1985 *New Horizons,* see Chronology.
 1988 *Influences,* see Chronology.

Owen, Louise
Dates Unavailable.
Group exhibitions:
 1986 *Black Women in View,* see Chronology.
 1986 *Tangled Roots: Mixed Media Exhibition,* see Chronology.

Pall, Waheed
b.1954, Place of Birth Unavailable.
Group exhibitions:
 1985 *New Horizons,* see Chronology.

1990 *In Focus,* see Chronology.
Reviews, articles, texts, etc.:
　　Waheed Pall, 'Reproduction: Durga', *Art & Artists,* no.225, (June 1985), 45.

Palmer, Eugene
b.1955, Kingston, Jamaica.
Solo exhibitions:
1988 *Sirens: Recent Paintings and Drawings by Eugene Palmer,* Bedford Hill Gallery, London.
1992 *Eugene Palmer: Recent Paintings,* Duncan Campbell Contemporary Art, London.
1993 *Eugene Palmer,* Norwich Gallery, Norwich [A Norwich Gallery and inIVA touring exhibition curated by Eddie Chambers and Lynda Morris].
Group exhibitions:
1985 *3rd Creation for Liberation,* see Chronology.
1986 *Caribbean Expressions in Britain,* see Chronology.
1987 *Creation for Liberation,* see Chronology.
1988 *Black Art: Plotting the Course,* see Chronology.
1991 *History and Identity: Seven Painters,* see Chronology.
1993 *Black People and the British Flag,* see Chronology.
1994 *Home and Away,* see Chronology.
Reviews, articles, texts, etc.:
　_ Rose Jennings, 'Eugene Palmer: 198 Gallery', *City Limits,* (28 June – 5 July 1990), 74.
　_ 'Eugene Palmer', *Black Arts in London,* no.125 (1 – 31 July 1990), 4, (198 Gallery, London).

Panchal, Shanti
b.1951, Gujarat, India.
Solo exhibitions:
1988 *Earthern Shades: Paintings by Shanti Panchal,* Cartwright Hall, Bradford.
Group exhibitions:
1985 *GLC Anti-Racist Mural Project,* see Chronology.
1986 *Twelve Days at the Roundhouse: Mural Artists,* see Chronology.
1989 *The Tree of Life,* South Bank Centre Touring Exhibition, London.
Reviews, articles, texts, etc.,
　_ Sally Jones, 'Shanti Panchal' [Square Gallery, London; exhibition], *Arts Review,* (16 November 1990), 622.
　_ David Lee, 'Viewpoints: Shanti Panchal: Royal Festival Hall, London', *Arts Review,* (August 1992), 339.
　_ Susan Morris, 'Shanti Panchal' [Chappel Galleries, England, and Artists in Education, Commonwealth Institute, London], *Arts Review,* (1 July 1988), 457.
　_ Frank Ruhrmund, 'Shanti Panchal' [Towner Art Gallery, Eastbourne, England; exhibition], *Arts Review,* (3 November 1989), 784.
　_ *Signs Of Resistance,* 1985: see Chronology.
　_ Gurminder Sikand, 'Earth Shades: Shanti Panchal', *Bazaar,* no.9, (1989),19-20.

Parmar, Pratibha
b.1955, Kenya.
Group exhibitions:
1987 *State of the Nation,* Herbert Art Gallery, Coventry.
1988 *Spectrum Women's Photography Festival Open Exhibition,* see Chronology.
1989 *Fabled Territories,* see Chronology.

1992 *White Noise,* see Chronology.
1992 *Who do you Take me for?,* see Chronology.
Texts by Prathiba Parmar:
1988 Prathiba Parmar, 'Emergence 2', in *Storms of the Heart,* edited by Kwesi Owusu,
(London: Camden Press, 1988), pp.47-54.
1990 Prathiba Parmar, 'Black Feminism: the Politics of Articulation' in *Identity: Community, Culture,*
Difference, edited by Jonathan Rutherford, (London: Lawrence & Wishart, 1990).
1992 Pratibha Parmar, 'Rage and Desire: Confronting Pornography', in *Addressing the Forbidden:*
Art Looks at Pornography, (Edinburgh: Stills), pp.11-14.
1984 Prathiba Parmar, 'Hateful Contraries: Media Images of Asian Women, *Ten.8,* no.16, 71-78,
(reprinted in *Ten.8: 'Critical Decade',* 2, no.3, (Spring 1992), 50-61).
Reviews, articles, etc.:
_ Suman Kumari Bhuchar, 'Chanelling the Anger: Pratibha Parmar', *Bazaar,* no.10, (1989), 3.
_ Meena Nanji, 'Pratibha Parmar', *High Performance,* 15, (Summer – Fall 1992), 28-29.
_ Ian Rashid, 'Leather and Silk and the Asian Lesbian Gaze' [interview], *Bazaar,* (Spring 1992), 24-25.
_ Cherry Smyth, Queer Questions, *Sight & Sound,* 2, (September 1992), 34-35.
_ Cherry Smyth, 'Pratibha Parmar Interviewed', *FAN-Feminist Art News,* 3, no.5, 2-5.

Patel, Anu
b.1961, Baroda, India.
Group exhibitions:
1985 *Eastern Views: Work by Young Asian Artists from the Midlands,* see Chronology.
1993 *Transition of Riches,* see Chronology.
Reviews, articles, texts, etc.:
_ Rose Jennings, 'A Brighter Prospect' (three projects that combine public art and the cultural
interests of the community), *Crafts,* no.117, (July – August 1992), 36-39.
_ Anu Patel, 'Untitled: Contorted Man' [Reproductions], *Art & Artists,* no.229, (October 1985), 47.

Patti, Symrath
b.1961, Place of Birth Unavailable.
Group exhibitions:
1986 *Jagrati,* see Chronology.
1989 *One Spirit: Black Artists against Racism,* see Chronology.
1993 *Transition of Riches,* see Chronology.
1993 *Renegotiations: Class, Modernity, and Photography,* Norwich Gallery, Norwich,
[Norfolk Institute of Art and Design, Norwich].
1994 *Quinta Bienal de la Habana,* see Chronology.
Reviews, articles, texts, etc.:
Symrath Patti, 'The Complete Promise', *Third Text,* no.19, (Summer 1992), 19-24.

Peries, Ivan
b.1921, Deriwala, Sri Lanka; died 1988, England.
Group exhibitions:
1989 *The Other Story,* see Chronology.
Reviews, articles, texts, etc.:
_ Senake Bandaranayake, 'Ivan Peries, (Paintings 1939-1969):
The Predicament of the Bourgeois Artist in the Societies of the Third World', *Third Text,* no.2,
(Winter 1987 – 1988), 76-92.
_ Ivan Peries, 'Dehiwala' (1978), *The Artist,* (February 1990), 3.

Phaophanit, Vongphuchun
b.1961, Laos.
Solo exhibitions:
1991 *Vong Phaophanit: What Falls to the Ground But Can't be Eaten,* Chisenhale Gallery, London.
Group exhibitions:
1989 *The Artist Abroad,* see Chronology.
1990 *The British Art Show,* see Chronology.
1990 *New Works For Different Places: TSWA Four Cities Project,* see Chronology.
1991 *Shocks to the System: Social and Political Issues in Recent British Art from the Arts Council Collection,* see Chronology.
1993 *Four Rooms,* see Chronology.
1993 *Ha-ha: Contemporary British Art in an 18th Century Park,* Killerton Park, Exeter.
1993 *The Turner Prize, 1993,* Tate Gallery, London.
1994 *From Beyond the Pale: Art and Artists at the Edge of Concensus,* Irish Museum of Modern Art, Dublin, pp.95.
1995 *Cocido y Crudo,* see Chronology.
1995 *Phaophanit and Piper,* see Chronology.
Reviews, articles, texts, etc.:
_ Kate Bush, 'Vong Phaophanit', *Flash Art,* no.171, (Summer 1993), 98.
_ *Installation Art,* edited by Nicolas De Oliveira...et al., (London: Thames & Hudson, 1994), pp.175.
_ Richard Dyer, 'Ash and Silk Wall', (Thames Barrier Garden, London; permanent installation), *Third Text,* no.26, (Spring 1994), 91-93.
_ Mark Griffin-Sherwood, 'Vong Phaophanit' [Arnolfini, Bristol], *Artscribe,* no.87, (Summer 1991), 64.
_ Tony Godfrey, 'Vong Phaophanit at Chisenhale', *Art in America,* (November 1991), 161, 175.
_ Brian Hatton, 'Umspace', *Art Monthly,* no.167, (June 1993), 19-21.
_ Simon Morrisey, 'Vong Phoaphanit and Keith Piper at Angel Row, Nottingham', *Untitled,* (Summer 1995), 13.
_ Adrian Searle, 'Fragments of Memory' [interview], *Frieze,* no.1, (1992), 20-23.
_ 'Turner Prize 1993', *Tate: The Art Magazine,* no.1, (Winter 1993), 48-55.

Phillips, Tony
b.1952, Liverpool, England.
Solo exhibitions:
1991 *Tony Phillips: Jazz and the Twentieth Century,* Ikon Gallery, Birmingham.
Group exhibitions:
1988 *Black Art: Plotting the Course,* see Chronology.
1991 *Four x 4,* see Chronology.
1991 *History and Identity: Seven Painters,* see Chronology.
1991 *Shocks to the System: Social and Political Issues in Recent British Art from the Arts Council Collection,* see Chronology.
Reviews, articles, texts, etc.:
Roger Malbert, 'Chronicles and Cautionary Tales: Tony Phillips' Jazz', *Art Monthly,* no.150, (October 1991), 23-24.

Piper, Keith
b.1960, Birmingham, England.

Solo exhibitions:

1984 *Past Imperfect/Future Tense: An Exhibition of Work by Keith Piper,* Black Art Gallery, London.
1987 *Another Empire State: An Exhibition of Work by Keith Piper,* Battersea Arts Centre, London, (poster, programmes and video documentation).
1988 *Chanting Heads: A Travelling Sculpture by Keith Piper,* Artangel Trust, London, (press release and card).
1991 *Keith Piper: Step Into The Arena – Notes on Black Masculinity & the Contest of Territory,* Rochdale Art Gallery, Rochdale.
1991 *A Ship Called Jesus,* Ikon Gallery, Birmingham.
1992 *Trade Winds: An Installation by Keith Piper,* (part of Trophies of Empire), see Chronology.

Group exhibitions:

1982 *The Pan-Afrikan Connection: an Exhibition of Work by Young Black Artists – Good Ideals,* see Chronology.
1983 *The Pan-Afrikan Connection,* see Chronology.
1983 *Heart in Exile,* see Chronology.
1984 *An Exhibition of Radical Black Art by the Blk Art Group,* see Chronology.
1984 *Into the Open,* see Chronology.
1985 *Black Skin/Bluecoat,* see Chronology.
1985 *From Generation to Generation (The Installation),* see Chronology.
1985 *GLC Anti-Racist Mural Project,* see Chronology.
1985 *New Horizons,* see Chronology.
1986 *Double Vision,* see Chronology.
1986 *From Two Worlds,* see Chronology.
1986 *New Contemporaries,* Institute of Contemporary Arts, London.
1986 *Unrecorded Truths,* see Chronology.
1987 *Art History: Artists Look at Contemporary Britain,* Hayward Gallery, London.
1987 *The Image Employed: The Use of Narrative in Black Art,* see Chronology.
1987 *OBAALA's Marcus Garvey Centenary Show,* see Chronology.
1987 *The Devil's Feast,* see Chronology.
1987 *State of the Nation,* Herbert Art Gallery & Museum, Coventry.
1988 *Changing Minds: Looking at Art Through Older Children's Eyes,* South Bank Centre, London.
1988 *The Essential Black Art,* see Chronology.
1988 *Influences,* see Chronology.
1989 *The Other Story,* see Chronology.
1990 *"Distinguishing Marks",* see Chronology.
1990 *Force 10: The Flag Project,* Glasgow District Council Festival and Project UK, Glasgow.
1991 *Black Markets,* see Chronology.
1991 *Interrogating Identity,* see Chronology.
1991 *Shocks to the System: Social and Political Issues in Recent British Art from the Arts Council Collection,* see Chronology.
1992 *Trophies of Empire,* see Chronology.
1994 *Quinta Bienal de la Habana,* see Chronology.
1994 *Us an' Dem,* see Chronology.
1995 *Cocido y Crudo,* see Chronology.
1995 *Freedom,* see Chronology.
1995 *Phaophanit and Piper,* see Chronology.
1995 *Video Positive 95: The UK's International Festival of Electronic Arts,* Moviola, Liverpool.
1996 *Boxer,* see Chronology.

Texts by Keith Piper:
1988 Keith Piper and Donald Rodney, 'Theory and practice', in *Storms of the Heart,*
       edited by Kwesi Owusu, (London: Camden Press, 1988), pp.113-118.
1990 'Chanting Heads: Keith Piper', (interviewed), *And-Journal of Art and Art Education,* no.21, 37-43.
1987 Keith Piper, 'Body and Text', *Third Text,* no.2, (Winter 1987 – 1988), 53-61.
1993 Keith Piper, 'Separate Spaces: A Personal Perspective on Black Art
       and the New Technologies', *Variant,* no.14, (Summer 1993), 8-11.
1993 Ameena Meer, 'Island Stories' [interview with Keith Piper], *Frieze,* no.6,
       (September – October 1993), 42-45.
Reviews, articles, etc.:
_ Dalya Alberge, 'Pick of the Day: Sculpture' ["Chanting heads" tour], 1988, *Independent,*
  (25 June 1988).
_ 'Another Empire State: an Exhibition of Work by Keith Piper' [Battersea Arts Centre],
  Black Arts in London, no.84, (1 – 25 October 1987), 16.
_ Michael Archer, 'Art History' [Hayward Gallery, London; exhibition], *Art Monthly,*
  (December – January 1988), 24-25.
_ John Byrne, 'Video Art Identity and the Processes of Cultural Mapping', *Variant,* no.14,
  (Summer 1993), 18-21.
_ Joyce Conor, 'Keith Piper/Kathy Prendergast' [Camden Arts Centre, London], *Art Monthly,*
  no.153, (February 1992), 20.
_ Sean Cubitt, 'Trade Winds' [Bluecoat Gallery, Liverpool: exhibition], *Hybrid,* pilot issue,
  (November – December 1992), 5.
_ Mark Currah, 'Battersea Arts Centre: Keith Piper', *City Limits,* (17 – 24 September 1987), 70-71.
_ Mark Currah, 'Piper Calls the Tune', *City Limits,* (29 October – 5 November 1987).
_ Jean Fisher, 'Keith Piper' [Bedford Hill Gallery, London], *Artforum,* (May 1989), 169-170.
_ Noelle Goldman, 'Chanting Heads in Public Places – Artangel Trust Focus on Multicultural
  UK', *Artswork – Greater London Newsletter,* no.20, (June – July 1988), 7-8.
_ 'Keith Piper: "A Ship Called Jesus"', *Revue Noire,* no.2, (September 1991), 22-24.
_ Keith Piper, 'Travelling Sculpture: "Chanting Heads"', *Arts Review,* (12 – 26 August 1988), 554.
_ Sarah Kent, 'New Contemporaries' [ICA: exhibit], *Time Out,* (19 – 25 March 1986), 33.
_ 'London Round-up: Keith Piper at The Black Art Gallery', *Art Monthly,* no.79,
  (September 1984), 22.
_ Kobena Mercer, 'Engendered Species' (Black Masculinity as seen by Danny Tisdale
  and Keith Piper), *Artforum,* (Summer 1992), 74-77.
_ Simon Morrisey, 'Vong Phaophanit and Keith Piper at Angel Row', Nottingham, *Untitled,*
  (Summer 1995), 13.
_ 'Multiracial UK' [Artangel Trust project "Chanting heads", 1988], *Performance,* no.53,
  (April – May 1988), 5.
_ 'Outside the Gallery', [Artangel Trust project "Chanting Heads", 1988], *AN-Artists Newsletter,*
  (June 1988), 18.
_ 'Keith Piper: Tagging the Other' (computer-processed video and electronic composite
  images, 1992), *Art in America,* (April 1994), 36.
_ 'Keith Piper: "Another Step into the Arena"', in *Masculine Masquerade: Masculinity
  and Representation,* edited by Andrew Perchuk and Helaine Posner,
  (Cambridge: Mass., MIT List Visual Arts Center, 1995), pp.116-117.
_ Nigel Pollitt, 'Past Imperfect, Future Tense by Keith Piper' [Black Art Gallery, London],
  City Limits, (22 – 28 June 1984), 70-71.
_ 'Donald Rodney & Keith Piper ["Adventures Close to Home", Pentonville Gallery, London],
  Time Out, (26 August – 2 September 1987), 29.
_ Amanda Sebestyen, 'Different Diasporas', *New Statesman & Society,* (3 February 1989), 49.
_ Caroline Smith, 'The Sample Art of Keith Piper' [interview], *Creative Camera,*
  (August – September 1995), 30-33.

Video Documentary:
1985 *Signs of Resistance,* see Chronology.
1989 Amanda Holiday, *Employing the Image: Making Spaces for Ourselves,* London.

Pollard, Ingrid
b.1953, Georgetown, Guyana.
Group exhibitions:
1985 *The Thin Black Line,* see Chronology.
1986 *Reflections of the Black Experience,* see Chronology.
1987 *D-Max,* see Chronology.
1987 *Polareyes,* see Chronology.
1989 *The Cost of the English Landscape,* see Chronology.
1989 *Intimate Distance,* see Chronology.
1990 *Disputed Identities,* see Chronology.
1990 *Heritage, Image, History,* see Chronology.
1990 *"Let the Canvas Come to Life with Dark Faces",* see Chronology.
1991 *Interrogating Identity,* see Chronology.
1992 *BBC Billboard Project,* see Chronology.
1995 *The Charge of The Light Brigade,* Bankspace, London.
1995 *Self-Evident,* see Chronology.
1996 *Boxer,* see Chronology.
Reviews, articles, texts, etc.:
_ 'Blackwomen's Creativity Project IV: Ingrid Pollard Photographs', in *Passion,* edited by Maud Sulter, (Hebden Bridge: Urban Fox Press, 1990), pp.19-43.
_ Tessa Boffin & Jean Fraser, 'Tantalizing Glimpses of Stolen Glances: Lesbians Take Photographs', *Feminist Review,* no.38, (Summer 1991), 20-32.
_ Sunil Gupta, 'Photography, Sexuality & Cultural Difference: the Emergence of Black Lesbian and Gay Identities in the UK', "Disputed Indentities", *SF Camerawork Quarterly,* 17, no.3, (Fall 1990), 19-26.
_ Ingrid Pollard, 'Another View' (photo-essay), *Feminist Review,* no.45, (Autumn 1993), 46-50.
_ 'Ingrid Pollard: Pastoral Interludes', *Third Text,* no.7, (Summer 1989), 41-46.
_ Kellie Jones, 'In their own Image' (Black Women Artists Who Combine Text With Photography), *Artforum,* (November 1990), 132-138.
_ 'Ingrid Pollard Talks to Molly Shinhat', *Polareyes,* no.1, (1987), 40-41.
_ 'Passion Profiles: Dionne Sparks, and Ingrid Pollard' [36 Martello Street, London E8; exhibition], *FAN-Feminist Art News,* 2, no.8, (1988), 20-21.
_ Yasmin Ramirez, 'Ingrid Pollard' [Art in General, New York; exhibition], *Art in America,* (October 1992), 144.
_ Mark Sealy, *Ingrid Pollard: Monograph,* (London: Autograph, 1995).
_ Gilane Tawadros, 'Other Britains, other Britons', *Aperture,* no.113, (Winter 1988), 40-46.

Povey, Ray
b.1947, England.
Group exhibitions:
1988 *Black Art: Plotting the Course,* see Chronology.
1989 *The Artist Abroad,* see Chronology.
1990 *"Let the Canvas Come to Life with Dark Faces",* see Chronology.

Purewal, Jaswinder Singh
b.1965, Coventry, England.
Group exhibitons:
1988 *Black Art: Plotting the Course,* see Chronology.
1990 *"Let the Canvas Come to Life with Dark Faces",* see Chronology.

Rahim, Sarah
b.1963, Sudan.
Group exhibitions:
1990 *"Let the Canvas Come to Life With Dark Faces",* see Chronology.
1993 *Black People and the British Flag,* see Chronology.

Rajah, Sher
b.1954, Pakistan.
Group exhibitions:
1988 *Sculptures by Amil Varia/Paintings by Sher Rajah/Paintings by Robin Davis,* Horizon Gallery, London.
1990 *"Let the Canvas Come to Life with Dark Faces",* see Chronology.
1990 *Mothers,* see Chronology.
1991 *Four x 4,* see Chronology.
1993 *Beyond Destination,* see Chronology.
1993 *Black People and the British Flag,* see Chronology.
1993 *The Phone Box: Art in Telephone Boxes,* (London: Virginia Nimarkoh/Bookworks, 1993).
1995 *The Art Casino: Risk Gambling and the National Lottery,* Barbican Art Gallery.
Reviews, articles, texts, etc.:
Prafulla Mohanti, 'Sher Rajah on the Horizon', *Artrage,* no.20, (Summer 1988), 33.

Rana, Samena
b.1958, Lahore, Pakistan; died 1992, London, England.
Group exhibitions:
1992 *Crossing Black Waters,* see Chronology.
1993 *Disrupted Borders,* see Chronology.
Reviews, articles, texts, etc.:
_ Shaheen Merali, 'Samena Rana: the Flow of Water', *Creative Camera,* no.319, (December – January 1993), 50-51.
_ 'Our Space in Britain', *Camerawork: Special Issue,* 1987.
_ Samena Rana, 'Disability and photography', *Polareyes,* no.1, (1987), 14-15.

Raphael, Alistair
b.1966, Dartford, England.
Group exhibitions:
1988 *Black Art: Plotting the Course,* see Chronology.
1988 *Numaish Lalit Kala,* see Chronology.
1990 *Post-morality,* see Chronology.
1991 *Four x 4,* see Chronology.
1994 *Hygiene: Writers and Artists Come Clean and Talk Dirty,* Ikon Gallery, Birmingham.
1995 *Sonia Boyce, Kary Kwok, Alistair Raphael: Free Stories,* L.A.Galerie, Frankfurt.
Reviews, articles, texts, etc.:
Sonali Fernando, 'Scaffolding of the Bone' [interview], *Bazaar,* no.22 (Autumn 1992), 7-9.

Roden, Suzanne
b.1958, Bournemouth, England.
Group exhibitions:
1986 *D-Max,* see Chronology.
1986 *Reflections of the Black Experience,* see Chronology.
1988 *Spectrum Women's Photography Festival Open Exhibition,* see Chronology.
Reviews, articles, texts, etc.:
'Autograph: Photo-Feature', *Artrage,* no.22/23, (Winter 1988), 29.

Rodney, Donald
b.1961, Birmingham, England.
Solo exhibitions:
1986 *The Atrocity Exhibition and Other Empire Stories: An Exhibition of Work by Donald Rodney,*
Black Art Gallery, London.
1989 *"Crisis": Donald Rodney,* Chisenhale Gallery, London, [press release and private view card].
1990 *Donald Rodney: Critical,* Rochdale Art Gallery, Rochdale, (texts by artist and Lubaina Himid).
1991 *Cataract,* Camerawork, London. [press release: Installation at Camerawork, London,
February – March 1991].
Group exhibitions:
1982 *The Pan-Afrikan Connection: an Exhibition of Work by Young Black Artists – Good Ideals,*
see Chronology.
1983 *The Pan-Afrikan Connection,* see Chronology.
1984 *An Exhibition of Radical Black Art by the Blk Art Group,* see Chronology.
1986 *Unrecorded Truths,* see Chronology.
1987 *Depicting History: For Today,* see Chronology.
1987 *The Devils Feast,* see Chronology.
1987 *The Image Employed: The Use of Narrative in Black Art,* see Chronology.
1987 *State of the Art,* see Chronology.
1987 *True Colours: The Red Wedge Visual Art Show,* Citizens Gallery, London.
1990 *"Let the Canvas Come to Life with Dark Faces",* see Chronology.
1990 *New Works for Different Places: TSWA Four Cities Project,* see Chronology.
1991 *Black Markets,* see Chronology.
1991 *Breaths: Art, Health and Empowerment,* Rochdale Art Gallery, Rochdale.
1991 *Interrogating Identity,* see Chronology.
1991 *Shocks to the System: Social and Political Issues in Recent British Art from the Arts Council
Collection,* see Chronology.
1992 *Us an' Dem,* see Chronology.
1993 *Borderless Print,* see Chronology.
1994 *Trophies of Empire,* see Chronology.
1994 *Truth Dare, Double Dare: Donald Rodney and Rose Finn-Kelcey,* Ikon Gallery, Birmingham.
1995 *Care and Control,* see Chronology.
Texts by Donald Rodney:
1988 Keith Piper and Donald Rodney, 'Theory and Practice', in *Storms of the Heart,*
edited by Kwesi Owusu, (London: Camden Press, 1988), pp.113-118.
Reviews, articles, etc.:
– Michael Archer, 'Collaborators', *Art Monthly,* no.178, (July – August 1994), 3-5.
– 'The Atrocity Exhibition and Other Empire Stories', *Black Arts in London,* no.60,
(16 – 31 July 1986), 8-9.
– 'The Atrocity Exhibition and Other Empire Stories', *Artrage,* no.13, (Summer 1986), 43.
– '*Crisis:* an Exhibition by Donald Rodney', *Black Arts in London,* no.111,
(1 February – 1 March 1989), 12, (Chisenhale Gallery, London).

_ Kwesi Owusu, 'Donald Rodney – Black Art With Cutting Edge', *Black Arts in London,* no.64, (16 – 31 October 1986), 3-5.
_ 'Donald Rodney & Keith Piper' [Pentonville Gallery, London; exhibition], *Time Out,* (26 August – 2 September 1987), 29.
_ Amanda Sebestyen, 'Different Diasporas', *New Statesman & Society,* (3 February 1989).
_ Noemi Smolik, 'Four Cities Project', *Kunstforum International,* Bd.111, (January – February 1991), 387-388.
_ Adeola Solanke, 'Donald Rodney' [Chisenhale Gallery, London; exhibition], *Art Monthly,* no.124, (March1989), 13-14.
_ 'Out of Town' (Arnolfini, Bristol; exhibition), *Black Arts in London,* no.125, (1 – 31 July 1990), 4.

Ryan, Veronica
b.1956, Monserrat.

Solo exhibitions:
1987 *Veronica Ryan: Sculpture,* Arnolfini Gallery, Bristol, [toured].
1987 *Veronica Ryan: Sculptures,* Castlefield Gallery, Manchester.
1988 *Veronica Ryan,* Kettle's Yard Gallery, Cambridge.
1988 *Veronica Ryan,* Riverside Studios, London.
1995 *Veronica Ryan: Compartments/Apart-ments*, Camden Arts Centre, London, (texts by Stella Santacatterina, the artist, and a facsimile of a letter to Veronica Ryan from Sonia Boyce).

Group exhibitions:
1983 *5 Black Women,* see Chronology.
1983 *International Drawing Biennale, 1983,* (Cleveland (UK) 6th international drawing biennale), Middlesbrough.
1984 *Into the Open: New Painting, Prints and Sculpture by Contemporary Black Artists,* see Chronology.
1985 *New Horizons,* see Chronology.
1985 *The Thin Black Line,* see Chronology.
1986 *Caribbean Expressions in Britain,* see Chronology.
1986 *From Two Worlds,* see Chronology.
1986 *Winter Exhibition: Lys Hansen, Lubaina Himid, Jayakumar, Jock McFadyen, Veronica Ryan, Andrew Walker,* Blond Fine Art, London.
1987 *Dislocations,* see Chronology.
1988 *Fire and Metal,* Goldsmiths' Gallery, London.
1990 *British Art Show,* McLellan Galleries, Glasgow.
1990 *New Necessity: First Tyne International 1990,* Gateshead.
1992 *Columbus Drowning,* see Chronology.
1993 *Recent British Sculpture from the Arts Council Collection,* London.

Reviews, articles, texts, etc.:
_ Mary Rose Beaumont, 'Veronica Ryan: Riverside Studios', *Arts Review,* (4 November 1988), 773.
_ Tony Godfrey, 'Recent Contemporary Sculpture Exhibitions', *Burlington Magazine,* (August 1984), 516.
_ Ian McKay, 'Veronica Ryan: Kettle's Yard, Cambridge', *Arts Review,* (2 December 1988), 877.
_ Robert Raczka, 'Veronica Ryan: The Wood Street Gallery, Pittsburgh', *New Art Examiner,* (September 1993), 37.
_ 'Veronica Ryan Artist in Residence at Kettle's Yard Talks to Clare Rendell', *Women Artists Slide Library Journal,* no.24, (August – September 1988) 15.
_ Tessa Sidey, 'Veronica Ryan: Wolverhampton Art Gallery', *Arts Review,* (2 May 1987), 345.

Sabharwal, Tara
b.1957, New Dehli, India.
Solo exhibitions:
1989 *Tara Sabharwal: Mylse Meehan Fellowship,* Myles Meehan Gallery, Darlington.
Group exhibitions:
1984 *Into the Open: New Painting, Prints and Sculpture by Contemporary Black Artists,*
see Chronology.
1988 *Revelations of Black,* see Chronology.
1990 *In Focus,* see Chronology.
Reviews, articles, texts, etc.:
Peter Inch, 'Tara Sabharwal', [Terrace Gallery, Harewood House, Leeds; exhibition],
Arts Review, (6 September 1991), 452.

Sambono, Charles
b.1953, Place of Birth Unavailable.
Solo exhibitions:
1987 *The Modern Eye of Africa: an Exhibition of Paintings by Charles Sambono,*
Commonwealth Institute, London.
Group exhibitions:
1986 *The Colours of Black,* see Chronology.
Reviews, articles, texts, etc.:
_ Ann Jones, 'Charles Sambono: Westbourne Gallery', *Arts Review,* (17 – 31 August 1984), 415.
_ David Lee, 'Charles Sambono: Westbourne Gallery, London', *Arts Review,* (9 May 1986),
247-248.

Sanderson, Lesley
b.1962, Malaysia.
Solo exhibitions:
1994 *These Colours Run: Lesley Sanderson,* (curated by Martin Barlow and Eddie Chambers,
texts by Gilane Tawadros and Jane Beckett), Wrexham Library Arts Centre touring exhibtion,
Bristol and Wrexham.
Group exhibitions:
1988 *Along the Lines of Resistance,* see Chronology.
1988 *Black Art: Plotting the Course,* see Chronology.
1990 *The British Art Show,* see Chronology.
1992 *Confrontations,* see Chronology.
1990 *New North: New Art from the North of Britain,* see Chronology.
1991 *Four x 4,* see Chronology.
1991 *History and Identity: Seven Painters,* see Chronology.
Reviews, articles, texts, etc.:
_ Emma Anderson, 'Four from Four x 4', *Women's Art Magazine,* no.44,
(January – February 1992), 12-13.
_ Rosemary Betterton, 'Lesley Sanderson', *Art Monthly,* no.184, (March 1995), 32-33.
_ Althea Greenan, 'Who Has the Last laugh?', *Women's Art Magazine,* no.61,
(November – December 1994), 23.
_ 'Visual Artist: Lesley Sanderson: Now you See me', *Blackboard Review,* no.2, (1990), 11.

Sang, Fitzroy
b.1955, Jamaica.
Group exhibitions:
1986 *The Colours Of Black,* see Chronology.
1987 *Creation for Liberation Open Exhibition,* see Chronology.
1990 *"Let the Canvas Come to Life with Dark Faces",* see Chronology.
Reviews, articles, texts, etc.:
_ '198 Gallery', *Black Arts in London,* no.121 (1 – 28 February 1991),10.
_ 'Imported Goods: On the Trail of the Serpent – an Exhibition of Paintings and Photographs by Fitzroy Sang' [Homerton Hospital Out Patients Department, London; exhibition], *Black Arts in London,* no.96, (16 – 30 April 1988), 4-6.

Sankofa Film Collective
est.1983
Reviews, articles, texts, etc.:
_ Martina Attille, 'The Passion of Remembrance; Background', *Framework,* no.32/33, 100-103.
_ Manthia Diawara, 'The Nature of Mother in "Dreaming Rivers"', *Third Text,* no.13, (Winter 1990 – 1991), 73-84.
_ Coco Fusco, 'An Interview with Martina Attille and Isaac Julien of Sankofa Film/Video Collective', in *Young, British and Black: the Work of Sankofa and Black Audio Film Collective,* by Coco Fusco, (Buffalo, NY.: Hallwalls/Contemporary Arts Center, 1988), pp.23-39.
_ Isiling Mack Natafi, 'Passion of Remembrance', *Spare Rib,* (December 1985), 22-26.
_ Jim Pines, 'The Passion of Remembrance' [interview with Sankofa], *Framework,* no.32/33, 92-99.
_ Jacob Ross, 'Passion of Remembrance: a Review', *Black Arts in London,* no.73, (1 – 15 April 1987), 3-5.

Shah, Tehmina
Pakistan, Dates Unavailable.
Group exhibitions:
1990 *Flowers East,* London.
1991 *A Table for Four,* see Chronology.
1994 *An Intelligent Rebellion: Women Artists of Pakistan,* Cartwright Hall, Bradford.
Reviews, articles, texts, etc.:
'Differences', *Black Arts in London,* no.36, (1 – 30 June 1991), 6.

Shemza, Anwar Jalal
b.1928, Simla, India.
Group exhibitions:
1989 *The Other Story,* See Chronology.
Reviews, articles, texts, etc.:
Mary Shemza 'Anwar Jalal Shemza: Search for Cultural Identity', *Third Text,* no.8/9, (Autumn – Winter 1989), 65-78.

Shoga, Folake
b.1955, Ibadan, Nigeria.
Group exhibitions:
1986 *Tangled Roots: Mixed Media Exhibition,* see Chronology.

1990 *"Let the Canvas Come to Life wtih Dark Faces"*, see Chronology.
1991 *Four x 4*, see Chronology.
1993 *Reclaiming the Madonna: Artists as Mothers*, see Chronology.
1994 *Seen|Unseen*, see Chronology.

Shonibare, Yinka
b.1962, London, England.
Group exhibitions:
1989 *Black Art: New Directions*, see Chronology.
1991 *Interrogating Identity*, see Chronology.
1994 *Seen|Unseen*, see Chronology.
1996 *Imagined Communities*, see Chronology.
Texts by Yinka Shonibare:
1994 Yinka Shonibare, 'Jean-Michel Basquiat, Please do not Turn in your Grave, its Only TENQ', *Third Text*, no.28/29, (Autumn – Winter 1994), 199-200.
Reviews, articles, etc.:
_ Okwui Enwezor, 'Occupied Territories: Power, Access and African Art' [Africa95], *Frieze*, no.26, (January – February 1996), 37-41.
_ Tania Guha, 'Yinka Shonibare: "Double Dutch"', *Third Text*, no.27, (Summer 1994), 87-90.
_ Kobena Mercer, 'Art that is Ethnic in Inverted Commas', *Frieze*, no.25, (November – December 1995), 38-41.

Sikand, Gurminder
b.1960, Jamshedpur, India.
Group exhibitions:
1985 *Eastern Views: Work by Young Asian Artists from the Midlands*, see Chronology.
1988 *Black Art: Plotting the Course*, see Chronology.
1990 *"Let the Canvas Come to Life with Dark Faces"*, see Chronology.
1992 *The Circular Dance*, see Chronology.
1992 *Fine Material for a Dream…?: A Reappraisal of Orientalism*, see Chronology.
1992 *Myths, Dream and Fable*, Angel Row Gallery, Nottingham.
Reviews, articles, texts, etc.:
Pauline Lucas, 'Eyes on the Body: Interview with Gurminder Sikand', *Womens Art Magazine*, no.62, (January – February 1995), 31.

Singh, Durlabh
b.1946, Kenya.
Group exhibitions:
1990 *"Let the Canvas Come to Life with Dark Faces"*, see Chronology.
Reviews, articles, texts, etc.:
_ 'Durlabh Singh: Image of Reality', *Artrage*, no.26, (Autumn 1989), 34, (Unwaged Centre, London, September 1989).
_ 'Unwaged Centre: "Images of Unreality"', *Black Arts in London*, no.117 (1 – 30 September 1989),11.

Smith, Marlene
b.1964, Birmingham, England.
Group exhibitions:
1983 *Heart In Exile*, see Chronology.
1984 *An Exhibition of Radical Black Art by the Blk Art Group*, see Chronology.
1986 *Unrecorded Truths*, see Chronology.
1987 *The Image Employed: The Use of Narrative in Black Art*, see Chronology.
1988 *Along the Lines of Resistance: An Exhibition of Contemporary Feminist Art*, see Chronology.
Reviews, articles, texts, etc.:
    Simone Alexander, 'Marlene Smith', *Artrage*, no.14, (Autumn 1986), 30.

Somerville, Elaine
Dates Unavailable.
Group exhibitions:
1986 *Black Women in View*, see Chronology.
1986 *Tangled Roots: Mixed Media Exhibition*, see Chronology.

Souza, Francis Newton
b.1924, Goa, India.
Solo exhibitions:
1959 *F.N.Souza*, Gallery One, London.
1961 *F.N.Souza*, Gallery One, London.
1962 *F.N.Souza*, Gallery One, London.
Group exhibitions:
1989 *The Other Story*, see Chronology.
Reviews, articles, texts, etc.:
    _ Geeta Kapur, 'Francis Newton Souza: Devil in the Flesh', *Third Text*, no.8/9, (Autumn – Winter 1989), 25-64.
    _ Edwin Mullins, *F.N.Souza*, (London: Blond, 1962).

Sparks, Dionne
b.1966, London, England.
Group exhibitions:
1989 *Black Art: New Directions*, see Chronology.
Reviews, articles, texts, etc.:
    _ '198 Gallery: Island Influences', *Black Arts In London*, no.119 (1 – 30 November 1989), 40-42.
    _ 'Passion Profiles: Dionne Sparks – Ingrid Pollard', *FAN-Feminist Art News*, 2, no.8, (1988), 20-21.
    _ Dionne Sparks, 'The Poetry of Theory', in *Passion*, edited by Maud Sulter, (Hebden Bridge: Urban Fox Press, 1990), pp.130-141.

Stephenson, Veena
b.1962, Kenya.
Group exhibitions:
1991 *A Table for Four*, see Chronology.
1993 *Black People and the British Flag*, see Chronology.
1994 *Trophies of Empire*, see Chronology.
Reviews, articles, texts, etc.:
    _ Rukhsana Mosam, 'Africa, our Africa', *Bazaar*, no.22, (Autumn 1992), 11.

_ Veena Stephenson, 'Can Someone Translate? I Want to Speak', *FAN-Feminist Art News,* 3,
no.6, 14-15.
_ Veena Stephenson, 'Rubbing Culture's Nose in the Mud of Politics', in *Passion,*
edited by Maud Sulter, (Hebden Bridge: Urban Fox Press, 1990), pp.121-129.

Stokes, Vincent
b.1964, England.
Group exhibitions:
1990 *Disputed Identities,* see Chronology.
1990 *"Let the Canvas Come to Life with Dark Faces",* see Chronology.
1991 *Four x 4,* see Chronology.
Reviews, articles, texts, etc.:
Bill Siepman, 'Castaways: Vincent Stokes', *Creative Camera,* no.323,
(August – September 1993), 16-17.

Suandi
Dates Unavailable.
Group exhibitions:
1988 *Once Upon a Time: An Exhibition of Pictures and Words by Black Women Artists,*
see Chronology.
1988 *Revelations of Black,* see Chronology.
Reviews, articles, texts, etc.:
_ 'Artists' pages … Suandi', in *Lets Get it On: The Politics of Black Performance,*
edited by Catherine Ugwu, (London: Institute of Contemporary Arts; Seattle:
Bay Press, 1995), pp.150-155.
_ Michael McMillan, 'A Voice in the Diaspora', *Hybrid,* no.5, (October – November 1993), 10-12.

Sulter, Maud
b.1960, Glasgow, Scotland.
Solo exhibitions:
1987 *Sphinx,* The Black Art Gallery, London, (publicity material).
1990 *Maud Sulter: Hysteria,* Tate Gallery, Liverpool and Brewery Arts Centre, Kendal,
(compact disc with catalogue).
1991 *Zabat,* Camerawork, London, (press release).
1994 *Maud Sulter: Syrcas,* Cyngor Sir Clywyd, Yr Wyddgrug, Wrexham Library Arts Centre,
touring exhibition, (text by Lubaina Himid).
Group exhibitions:
1985 *3rd Creation for Liberation,* see Chronology.
1985 *The Thin Black Line,* see Chronology.
1987 *New Robes for MaShulan,* see Chronology.
1988 *Along the Lines of Resistance: An Exhibition of Contemporary Feminist Art,*
see Chronology.
1989 *Black Art: New Directions,* see Chronology.
1990 *New North: New Art from the North of Britain,* see Chronology.
1991 *Shocks to the System: Social and Political Issues in Recent British Art from the Arts Council
Collection,* see Chronology.
1992 *Columbus Drowning,* see Chronology.
1990 *Treatise on the Sublime,* see Chronology.
1993 *Borderless Print,* see Chronology.

1994 *Intimate Lives: Photographers and their Families,* Focal Point Gallery, Southend-on-Sea
and Cambridge Darkroom, Cambridge.

Texts by Maud Sulter:

1989 Maud Sulter, *As a Blackwoman: Poems 1982 – 1985,*
(Hebden Bridge: Urban Fox Press, 1989).

1985 Maud Sulter, 'Blackwomen's Creativity Project', *Gen,* (October – December 1985), 51-52,
and *Gen,* no.7/8, (1986), 58-59.

1988 Maud Sulter, 'Call and Response', *FAN-Feminist Art News,* 2, no.8, 15-17.

1989 Maud Sulter, *Zabat,* (Hebden Bridge, Urban Fox Press, 1989).

1990 *Claudette Johnson: Pushing Back the Boundaries,* see artist's listing.

1990 Maud Sulter, 'The Making Of Necropolis: The Text as a Site of Cultural Struggle',
FAN-Feminist Art News, 3, no.4, 20.

1990 *Passion: Discourses on Blackwomen's Creativity,* edited by Maud Sulter,
(Hebden Bridge, Urban Fox Press,1990), [essays by Maud Sulter include: 'Blackwomen's
Creativity Project: an Overview', 'Talking in Tongues', 'Poetics of a Family Tree – Extracts',
'Section Three: Portfolio – Lubaina Himid & Maud Sulter', and 'Empowerment'].

1991 Maud Sulter, 'Earlestown: Merseyside Cityline', *FAN-Feminist Art News,* 3, no.7, 11-14.

1991 *Echo: Works by Women Artists, 1850 – 1940,* Tate Gallery, Liverpool,
(text and selection by Maud Sulter).

1991 Maud Sulter, 'Artists of a Diaspora: Talking to Myself Again', *Alba,* 1, no.4,
(August – September 1991), 16-17.

1992 *The Fortune Teller: Karen Knorr, Lorna Simpson and Olivier Richon,* Rochdale Art Gallery,
Rochdale.

1992 Maud Sulter, 'Without Tides, No Maps', in *Lubaina Himid: Revenge,* Rochdale Art Gallery.

Reviews, articles, etc.:

_ Sarah Bayliss, 'Maud Sulter', [Steinbaum Krauss Gallery, New York; exhibition],
Art in America, (May 1993), 120-121.

_ Jane Beckett & Deborah Cherry, 'A Limitless Sublimity: The Art of Lubaina Himid
and Maud Sulter', in *Treatise on the Sublime,* (Stanislaus: University of Caifornia,
University Gallery), 1990, pp.2-3.

_ Robert Clark, 'Maud Sulter: Photoworks' [Rochdale Art Gallery, Rochdale: exhibition],
The Guardian, (23 October 1989).

_ Ann Cullis, 'Missing: Presumed Black: Maud Sulter at the Ikon Gallery' [*Hysteria*: exhibition],
Creative Camera, no.314, (February – March 1992), 45-46.

_ Mark Currah, 'Black Art Gallery – Maud Sulter', *City Limits,*
(26 November – 3 December 1987), 69.

_ 'Echo and Hysteria', *Black Arts in London,* no.137, (July 1991), 26, (Tate, Liverpool).

_ *From Beyond the Pale: Art and Artists at the Edge of Concensus,*
Irish Museum of Modern Art, Dublin, 1994, pp.97.

_ 'Gold Blooded Warrior: New Work by Lubaina Himid and Maud Sulter', *Black Arts in London*,
no.97, (1 – 15 May 1988), 13. (Tom Allen Centre, London).

_ Mark Haworth-Booth, 'Maud Sulter: An Interview', *History of Photography,* 16,
(Autumn 1992), 263-266.

_ David Lillington, 'Maud Sulter: Camerawork', *Time Out,* (3 – 10 April 1991), 41.

_ 'Maud Sulter: Alba at the Centre for Contemporary Arts', in *Fotofeis: International Festival
of Photography in Scotland,* edited by Alistair Foster…et al., Fotofeis, Edinburgh, 1995,
pp.86-87.

_ Maud Sulter, 'Helas l'Heroine' (1993), *Women's Art Magazine,* no.59, (1994), 10.

_ Maria Lind, 'Maud Sulter: Syrcas', *Portfolio,* no.19, (1994), 4-9 & 42-43.

_ Maud Sulter, 'Zabat Series' [untitled],*Creative Camera,* no.6, (October – November 1990),46.

_ Lorna J.Waite, 'Maud Sulter: Syrcas', *Creative Camera,* no.330, (October– November 1994), 38.

_ Maxine Walker, 'Testimony: Three Black Women Photographers',

[Camerawork, London; exhibition], *Creative Camera,* no.4, (1987), 34.
_ 'Zabat at Camerawork', *Black Arts in London,* no.135 (1 – 30 April 1991), 7.

Tabrizian, Mitra
b.1952, Iran.
Group exhibitions:
1984 *The Selectors' Show,* see Chronology.
1986 *Mitra Tabrizian, Victor Burgin, Mari Mahr,* The Photographers Gallery, London.
1991 *Shocks to the System: Social and Political Issues in Recent British Art from the Arts Council Collection,* see Chronology.
1992 *Fine Material for a Dream...?: A Reappraisal of Orientalism,* see Chronology.
Texts by Mitra Tabrizian:
1984 Mitra Tabrizian, 'College of Fashion/Modelling Course', *Creative Camera,* no.232, (April 1984), 1327-1331.
1987 'The Blues: An Interview with Mitra Tabrizian', *Ten.8,* no.25, 30-35.
1990 Mitra Tabrizian, *Correct Distance,* (Manchester: Cornerhouse, 1990).
Reviews, articles, etc.:
_ Robert Hamilton, 'Beyond the Purloined Image: at Riverside', *Artscribe,* no.43, (October 1983), 60-61.
_ Kellie Jones, 'In Their Own Image', *Artforum,* (November 1990), 132-138.
_ David Lee, 'Photography', *Arts Review,* 43, (28 June 1991), 321-322.
_ Laura Mulvey, 'Magnificent Obsession', *Parachute,* no.42, (March – May 1986), 6-12.
_ Griselda Pollock, *Vision and Difference: Femininity, Feminism and Histories of Art,* (London: Routledge, 1988), pp.171-174.
_ Randi Saharuni, 'Racism and Photography', *C Magazine,* no.18, (Summer 1988), 33-35.
_ Mitra Tabrizian, 'Correct Distance', *Creative Camera,* no.256, (April 1986), 20-28.
_ Michael Tarantino, 'The Other Body', *Artforum,* (February 1988), 150-151.
_ Gilane Tawadros, 'Other Britains, other Britons', *Aperture,* no.113, (Winter 1988), 40-46.

Tang, Lin
Dates Unavailable.
Group exhibitions:
1988 *Once Upon a Time: An Exhibition of Pictures and Words by Black Women Artists,* see Chronology.
1988 *Revelations of Black,* see Chronology.

Thomas, Shanti
b.1949, London, England.
Solo exhibitions:
1987 *An exhibition of Paintings and Drawings by Shanti Thomas,* Bhownagree Gallery, Commonwealth Institute, London.
Group exhibitions:
1986 *Jagrati,* see Chronology.
1987 *Critical Realism: Britain in the 1980's through the Work of 28 Artist,* see Chronology.
1988 *Black Art: Plotting the Course,* see Chronology.
1989 *The Artist Abroad,* see Chronology.
1990 *In Focus,* see Chronology.
1990 *"Let the Canvas Come to Life with Dark Faces",* see Chronology.
1992 *The Circular Dance,* see Chronology.

Texts by Shanti Thomas:
1993 Shanti Thomas, 'Rootless', *FAN-Feminist Art News,* 4, no.5, 6.
Reviews, articles, etc.:
– David Lee, 'Shanti Thomas', [Commonwealth Institute, London; exhibition], *Arts Review,* (8 May 1987), 297-298.
– Nadir Tharani, 'Shanti Thomas' [Bhownagree Gallery, Commonwealth Institute, London; exhibition], *Artrage,* no.17, (Summer 1987), 48.

Thompson, Gladstone
b.1959, London, England.
Solo exhibitions:
1993 *Gladstone Thompson: A Work Made at the Cairn Gallery,* Cairn Gallery, Nailsworth.
Group exhibitions:
1991 *Present Continuous,* Artsite Trust, Bath.
1992 *Etats spécifiques,* Musée des Beaux-Arts André Malraux, Le Havre.
1993 *Four Rooms,* see Chronology.
1994 *De Ateliers 1985 – 1993,* De Ateliers, Amsterdam.
1995 *Krijn De Koning/Gladstone Thompson,* Establissements d'en Face, Bruxelles.
Reviews, articles, texts, etc.:
– Jean-Charles Agboton-Jumeau, 'Gladstone Thompson', [Galerie des Archives, Paris], *Forum International,* 3, no.13, (May – August 1992), 90.
– 'Four Rooms', *Art & Design Profile,* [Installation Art], no.30, (1993).

Uddin, Shafique
b.1962, Beani Bozar, Bangladesh.
Solo exhibitions:
1988 *Shafique Uddin,* Horizon Gallery, London.
1991 *Shafique Uddin: Recent Paintings,* Terrace Gallery, London.
Group exhibitions:
1986 *Brushes With The West,* see Chronology.
1986 *From Two Worlds,* see Chronology.
1987 *In Another World: Outsider Art from Europe & America,* Ferens Art Gallery, Hull, (organized by the South Bank Centre, London).
1988 *Numaish Lalit Kala,* see Chronology.
1990 *The British Art Show,* see Chronology.
1990 *In Focus,* see Chronology.
Reviews, articles, texts, etc.:
Allan de Souza, 'Shafique Uddin' [Rebecca Hossack, London: exhibition], *Bazaar,* (Summer 1992), 23.

Varia, Anil
b.1964, Place of Birth Unavailable.
Group exhibitions:
1988 *Sculptures by Amil Varia/Paintings by Sher Rajah/Paintings by Robin Davis,* Horizon Gallery, London.
1990 *In Focus,* see Chronology.
Reviews, articles, texts, etc.:
Tim Moock, 'Anil Varia', [Horizon Gallery, London; exhibition], *Arts Review,* (15 July 1988), 490-491.

Venair, Aldith
Dates Unavailable.
Group exhibitions:
1988 *Once Upon a Time: An Exhibition of Pictures and Words by Black Women Artists,*
see Chronology.
1988 *Revelations of Black,* see Chronology.

Vernon, Janet
Dates Unavailable.
Group exhibitions:
1983 *The Pan-Afrikan Connection,* see Chronology.

Wagh, Ibrahim
b.1936, India.
Group exhibitions:
1990 *In Focus,* see Chronology.
1990 *"Let the Canvas Come to Life with Dark Faces",* see Chronology.

Walker, Kanta
Dates Unavailable.
Solo exhibitions:
1989 *Jug-Mug-Jugni: Paintings by Kanta Walker,* Oldham Art Gallery, Oldham.
Group exhibitions:
1988 *Revelations of Black,* see Chronology.
Reviews, articles, texts, etc.:
_ 'Jug-Mug-Jugni', *Black Arts in London,* no.112, (1 – 31 March 1989), 12.
_ Kanta Walker, 'Conquerors and Explorers', *FAN-Feminist Art News,* 3, no.1, 16-17.

Walker, Maxine
b.1962, Birmingham, England.
Group exhibitions:
1989 *Intimate distance,* see Chronology.
1995 *Self-Evident,* see Chronology.
Texts by Maxine Walker:
1987 Maxine Walker, 'Boxed Gems', *Polareyes,* no.1, 42-43.
1987 Maxine Walker, 'We do not Wish to Do it Quietly', *Ten.8,* no.27, 42-45.
1990 Maxine Walker, 'Beauty and the Beast: Have Images of Black Women in the Media Changed
over the Years?', *Blackboard Review,* no.2, 12-13.
1991 Maxine Walker, 'Intimate Distance', in *Family Snaps,* edited by Jo Spence
and Patricia Holland, (London: Virago, 1991), pp.222-225.
Reviews, articles, etc.:
_ Joy Gregory, 'Fantasy: Joy Gregory Speaking to Maxine Walker', *Polareyes,* no.1, (1987), 18-19.
_ 'Portfolio: Maxine Walker', *Creative Camera,* no.8/9, (1987), 42-43.
_ Gilane Tawadros, 'Redrawing the Boundaries: The Documentary Work of David Lewis
and Maxine Walker', *Ten.8: 'Critical Decade',* 2, no.3, (Spring 1992), 86-92.

Walsh, Geraldine
b.1961, England.
Group exhibitions:
1987 *Polareyes,* see Chronology.
1988 *Contemporary Art by Afro-Caribbean Artists,* see Chronology.
1990 *"Let the Canvas Come to Life with Dark Faces",* see Chronology.
Reviews, articles, texts, etc.:
_ Geraldine Walsh, 'Celebrating Having the Joys of Having a Grandmother…', *Polareyes,* no.1, (1987), pp.24-25.

Wandja, Jan
b.1950, London, England.
Group exhibitions:
1987 *State of the Nation,* Herbert Art Gallery, Coventry.
1988 *Black Art: Plotting the Course,* see Chronology.
Reviews, articles, texts, etc.:
_ Michael Newman, 'Simulcra', *Flash Art,* no.110, (January 1983), 38-40.
_ Rosetta Brooks, 'From the Night of Consumerism to the Dawn of Simulation', *Artforum,* (February 1985), 76-81.

Wanogho, Enyote
Dates Unavailable.
Group exhibitions:
1985 *Mirror Reflecting Darkly,* see Chronology.
1986 *Tangled Roots: Mixed Media Exhibition,* see Chronology.

Williams, Aubrey
b.1926, Georgetown, Guyana; died 1990.
Solo exhibitions:
1985 *The Olmec-Maya & Now: New Work by Aubrey Williams,* Commonwealth Institute, London.
1995 *Aubrey Williams' "Cosmos" Series,* The October Gallery, London.
Group exhibitions:
196? *Four Commonwealth Painters,* Arts Centre, University of Sussex, Brighton.
1971 *Caribbean Artists in England,* see Chronology.
1973 *Eight Commonwealth Artists,* see Chronology.
1985 *Creation for Liberation,* see Chronology.
1986 *Caribbean Expressions in Britain,* see Chronology.
1986 *The Colours of Black,* see Chronology.
1989 *The Other Story,* see Chronology.
1995 *The Caribbean Connection,* see Chronology.
Reviews, articles, texts, etc.:
_ Rauf Adu, 'The Mark of the Hand of the Man', *Artrage,* no.15, (Winter 1986), 37.
_ Rasheed Araeen, 'Conversation with Aubrey Williams', *Third Text,* no.2, (Winter 1987 – 1988), 25-52.
_ Oswell Blakeston, 'Aubrey Williams: October Gallery', *Arts Review,* (28 September 1984), 473.
_ Denis Bowen, 'Aubrey Williams',[obituary], *Art Monthly,* no.137,(June 1990), 35.
_ Guy Brett, 'Aubrey Williams' [obituary], *The Independent,* (1 May 1990).
_ Sue Hubbard, 'Aubrey Williams', *Time Out,* (17 – 24 January 1996), 48.

_ David Lee, 'Aubrey Williams', [October Gallery, London; exhibition], *Arts Review*, (5 June 1987), 381-382.
_ Errol Lloyd, 'Aubrey Williams: Myth and Symbol', *Artrage*, no.9/10, (Autumn 1985), 4-5.
_ Geoffrey Maclean, 'Tapping the Source', *Caribbean Beat Magazine*, (Winter 1992 – 1993).
_ 'October Gallery: Aubrey Williams', *Black Arts in London*, no.119, (1 – 30 November 1989), 9.

Williams, Paula
Dates Unavailable.
Group exhibitions:
1985 *Mirror Reflecting Darkly*, see Chronology.
1986 *Black Women in View*, see Chronology.
1986 *Tangled Roots: Mixed Media Exhibition*, see Chronology.

Zaidi, Ali Mehdi
b.1963, Dates Unavailable.
Group exhibitions:
1990 *Post-morality*, see Chronology.
1991 *Jashan-E-Bahar*, see Chronology.
1993 *Captives*, see Chronology.

General Texts

Visual art practice

Araeen, Rasheed
_ 'The Emergence of Black Consciousness in Contemporary Art in Britain:
Seventeen Years of Neglected History' in *The Essential Black Art,*
(London: Chisenhale Gallery, 1988), pp.5-11.
_ *Making Myself Visible,* (London: Kala Press, 1984).
_ 'Preliminary Notes for a Black Manifesto', *Black Phoenix,* no.1, (Winter 1978), 3-12.
Araeen, Rasheed and Eddie Chambers
'Black Art: A Discussion', *Third Text,* no.5, (Winter 1988 – 1989), 51-77.
Arup, Evie
'Black Art is the Only Art', *The Weekly Journal,* (20 July 1995), 12.

Biswas, Sutapa
'The Presence of Black Women', *Art Monthly,* (February 1989), 11.
The Black Experience Arts Programme
(London: Greater London Council, Race Equality Unit, 1986).
'Black Visual Artists Forum: A Programme of Seminars and Workshops'
Black Arts in London, no.64, (16 – 31 October 1986), 9-10.
**Black Women Artists Today: A Series of Five Seminars Looking at the Work of Black Women
in the Visual Arts**
Brixton Village, London, June – July 1988, (press release and programme).
'Blackwomen's Creativity'
FAN-Feminist Art News, Special Issue, edited by Lubaina Himid and Maud Sulter, 2, no.8,
(Autumn 1988).
Bowling, Frank
'Formalist Art and the Black Experience', *Third Text,* no.5, (Winter 1988 – 1989), 78-94.
Burman, Chila
'There Have Always Been Great Blackwomen Artists', in *Visibly Female, Feminism and Art:
an Anthology*, edited by Hilary Robinson, (London: Camden Press, 1987), pp.195-199,
(earlier version produced as an unpublished paper in 1986 for the Greater London Council
Race Equality Unit).

Chambers, Eddie
'The Black Art Group', *Artrage,* no.14, (Autumn 1986), 28-29.

Extending Frontiers: Black Artists at Work
(Bradford: Yorkshire Arts, 1988).

Fernando, Sonali
'Hair of the Dog? Perspectives on Artists of South Asian Descent in Britain', *Fuse,* 18, no.1, 16-25.

Himid, Lubaina
_ 'Attention Young Black Artists', *Art Monthly,* no.61, (November 1982), 18.
_ 'Fragments: An Exploration of Everyday Black Creativity and its Relationship to Political Change',
FAN-Feminist Art News, 2, no.8, (1988), 8-9.
_ 'In the Woodpile: Black Women Artists and the Modern Woman', *FAN-Feminist Art News,* 3, no.4, 2-3.
_ 'Mapping: A Decade of Black Women Artists', in *Passion: A Discourse on Blackwomen's Creativity,*
edited by Maud Sulter, (Hebden Bridge: Urban Fox Press, 1990), pp.62-72.
_ 'We Will Be', in *Looking on: Images of Femininity in the Visual Arts and Media,*
edited by Rosemary Betterton, (London: Pandora Press, 1987), pp.259-266.

Holiday, Amanda
  Employing the Image: Five Artists in Britain who Produce Issue Based Work: Simone Alexander,
  Sonia Boyce, Zarina Bhimji, Keith Piper and Allan de Souza, London, 1989, (video).

Jantjes, Gavin
  'Critical Perspectives: The Role of the Visual Artist', *Artrage,* no.2, (February 1983), 2-3.
Johnson, Claudette
  African Women: Reclaiming our Lives, (unpublished BA dissertation, Wolverhampton
  Polytechnic, n.d.).

Khan, Naseem
  'The Arts of Ethnic Minorities in Britain', *Journal of the Royal Society of Arts,* (September 1980),
  676-688.

La Rose, John
  'Black Artists in Britain', *Race Today Review,* (1985) 39, 41.
Lucie-Smith, Edward
  Race, Sex, and Gender in Contemporary Art: The Rise of Minority Culture, (London: Art Books
  International, 1994).

Owusu, Kwesi
  _ 'Unsung Innovators', *New Statesman,* (23 May 1986), 22-24.
Owusu, Kwesi and Jacob Ross
  _ 'Black Arts: Defining an Agenda', in *Looking Beyond the Frame: Racism, Representation and
  Resistance,* edited by Michelle Reeves, Jenny Hammond, (Oxford: Links 34, 1989), pp.39-43.

Piper, Keith
  'Black Art: A Statement', in *The Essential Black Art,* (London: Chisenhale Gallery, 1988),
  pp.46-47.

Ramamurthy, Anandi
  'Spilling over Margins: the Question of Categorisation for South Asian Artists', *Artrage,* no.18,
  (Autumn 1987), 6-7.
Reedy, Carlyle
  'Marginalisation' [correspondence], *Art Monthly,* no. 86, (May 1985), 24.

Storms of the Heart: An Anthology of Black Arts and Culture
  Edited by Kwesi Owusu, (London: Camden Press, 1988).
Streete, Delta
  'In the Deep: An Elbow Room Commission', *FAN-Feminist Art News,* 3, no. 4, 16-17.
Suandi
  'Black Arts Alliance', *Artists Newsletter,* (October 1991), 35.
Sulter, Maud
  _ 'Blackwomen's Creativity Project', *Gen,* (October – December 1985), 51-52, and *Gen,* no. 7/8,
  (1986), 58-59.
  _ 'A Portrait of the Artist as Poor, Black and a Woman', in *Glancing Fires: An Investigation into
  Women's Creativity,* edited by Lesley Saunders (London: The Women's Press, 1987), pp.148-155.

Tawadros, Gilane
  _ 'Beyond the Boundary: The Work of Three Black Women Artists in Britain' [Lubaina Himid,
  Sonia Boyce and Sutapa Biswas], *Third Text,* no. 8/9, (Autumn – Winter 1989), 121-150.
  _ 'The Sphinx Contemplating Napoleon: Black Women Artists in Britain',

in *New Feminist Art Criticism: Critical Strategies,* edited by Katy Deepwell, (Manchester: Manchester University Press, 1995), pp.25-30.
Taylor, Stuart
'The Free Lunch: Five Artists of Asian and African-Caribbean Origin Discuss their Experiences of Living and Working in Britain' [Stuart Taylor, Delta Streete, Alistair Raphael, Andrew Calaya Chetty and Esther White], *Hybrid,* no.1, (February – March 1993), 12-15.

'View From the Archive: Black Women Artists Index'
Women Artists Slide Library Journal, no.33, (March – April 1990), 17-19.

'Wild Women Shock Art'
Blackboard Review, Special Issue, no. 2, (1990). ·
Woodley, Karin
'Association of London Black Artists (ALBA)', *Black Arts in London*, no. 46, (15 December – 15 January 1986), 6.

Photography: theory and practice
Akomfrah, John
'On the Borderline', *Ten.8,* 2, no.1, (1991), 51-67.

Bailey, David A.
– 'The Black Subject at the Centre: Repositioning Black Photography',
in *Looking Beyond The Frame: Racism, Representation and Resistance,*
edited by Michelle Reeves, Jenny Hammond, (Oxford: Links 34, 1989), pp.31-37.
– 'Explorations of Black Imagery', *Artrage,* (Summer 1986), 24-25.
– 'New Agendas within Black Cultural Politics', *Ten.8,* no. 22, 2-4.
– 'Photography and Black Communities', *AN-Artists Newsletter,* (August 1986), 20-21.
– 'Re-thinking Black Representation: from Positive Images to Cultural Photographic Practices',
Ten.8, no.31, (Winter 1988), 36-49.
– 'Positive Images', *AN-Artists Newsletter,* (July 1987), 22.
Bailey, David A. and Stuart Hall
'The Vertigo of Displacement: Shifts within Black Documentary Practices' [images by Dave Lewis, Vanley Burke and Franklyn Rodgers], *Ten.8: Critical Decade,* 2, no.3, (Spring 1992), 14-23.
Bishton, Derek
'Under the Skin', [the Sidelines Project in Birmingham],*Ten.8,* no.7/8, 12-17.
'Black Experiences'
Ten.8, Special Issue, no. 22.
'Black Photographers Association'
Creative Camera, no.10, (1988), 7.

Chambers, Eddie
'In our own Image' [D-Max project], *GLA Quarterly,* 8, (Spring 1987), 28-29.
Coker, Simiola and Devdan Sen
African Caribbean & South Asian Photography Project [report],
(London: The Arts Council of Great Britain and the Minorities Arts Advisory Service, 1986).

Fernando, Sonali
'Blackened Images', *Bazaar,* no.12, 14-16.
Francis, Errol and Kobena Mercer
'Black People, Culture and Resistance', *Camerawork,* (November 1982), 6-8.

Gupta, Sunil
_ 'Autograph Photographers', *Artists Newsletter,* (December 1989), 31.
_ 'Desire and Black Men', *Ten.8,* no.22, 16-23.

Hall, Stuart
_ 'Identity and the Black Photographic Image' [images by Armet Francis,
Joy Gregory and Vincent Stokes], *Ten.8: Critical Decade,* 2, no.3, (Spring 1992), 24-31.
_ 'Reconstruction work: Images of Post-War Settlement', *Ten.8,* no.16, 2-8,
(reprinted in *Family Snaps,* edited by Jo Spence and Patricia Holland, (London: Virago, 1991),
pp.52-164; and *Ten.8: Critical Decade,* 2, no. 3, (Spring 1992), 106-113).

Hirst, Alex
'Black & Beyond', *Creative Camera,* no.316, (June – July 1992), 30-34.

Jones, Kellie
'Recreations: Black/Migrant Women Photographers' [Roshini Kempadoo, Ingrid Pollard,
Mitra Tabrizian and Zarina Bhimji], *Ten.8: Critical Decade,* 2, no.3, (Spring 1992), 96-106.

Julien, Isaac and Kobena Mercer
'True Confessions: A Discourse on Images of Black Male Sexuality', *Ten.8,* no. 22, (1986), 4-9
(reprinted in *Ten.8: Critical Decade*, 2, no.3, (Spring 1992), 40-49).

Mercer, Kobena
_ 'Dark & Lovely: Notes on Black Gay Image-Making', *Ten.8,* 2, no.1, (Spring1991), 78-85.
_ 'Mis(sed) Representations: Sickle Cell Autograph', *Black Arts In London,* no. 116, (1 – 31 July 1989),
12 (Association of Black Photographers, London).

Parmar, Pratibha
_ 'Hateful Contraries/Transistory Moments', *Ten.8: Critical Decade,* 2, no.3, (Spring 1992), 50-61.
_ 'Transitory Movements', in *Spectrum Women's Photography Festival Catalogue: A Collaboration
with Ten.8,* (1988), 8-11.

Patel, Amina and Laxmi Jamdagni
'Black Lives: White Careers', *FAN-Feminist Art News,* no. 6, 16-17.

Polareyes
A Journal by and about Black Women Working in Photography, no.1, (1987).

Rana, Samena
_ 'Disability and Photography', *FAN-Feminist Art News,* 2, no.10, 22-23.
_ 'Racism and Photography', *C Magazine,* no.18, (June 1988), 33-35.

Solanke, Adeola
'Complex, Not Confused', in *Family Snaps,* edited by Jo Spence and Patricia Holland,
(London: Virago,1991), pp.128-138.

Sparks, Dionne
'Looking at *Picture That'*, *FAN-Feminist Art News,* 3, no.6, 31-32.

Tawadros, Gilane
_ 'Other Britains, other Britons', *Aperture,* no.113, (Winter 1988), 40-46.
_ Who Needs Anti-racist Approaches to Photography: An Educational Pack Reviewed', *Ten.8,*
no.34, (Autumn 1989), 48-51.

'Towards a Documentation of Black Arts in Britain'
Artrage, no.16, (Spring 1987), 19, (Review of African, Caribbean & South Asian photography
by Similola Coker & Devdan Sen).

Walker, Maxine
'We do not Wish to do it Quietly' [*Polareyes* magazine], *Ten.8,* no.27, 42-45.
Wauchope, Sandra
'Photography: The Family Photo Album and Education', *FAN-Feminist Art News,* 3, no.6, 19-20.
Wilson, Rhonda
'Reading, Writing & Representation' [interview with Richard Gagola], *Ten 8,* no.28, 44-53.

Film & video: theory and practice
Anti-Racist Film Programme
(London: Greater London Council, 1984).
Anti-Racist Film Programme: Cinema Circuit
(London: Greater London Council, 1985).

Bhuchar, Suman Kumari
'Take Three Women: Asian Women are Calling the Shots behind the Camera',
Blackboard Review, no.2, (1990), 19-21.
'Black and Asian Film-Makers Skills Development Research Study'
London Film and Video News, 5, (November/December 1995 – January 1996).
Black and Third World Film Programme
(London: Greater London Council, Race Equality Unit,1986).
Black Film, British Cinema
Edited by Kobena Mercer, ICA Document 7, (London: Institute of Contemporary Arts, 1988).
Blackframes: Critical Perspectives on Black Independent Cinema
Edited by Mbye B. Cham and Claire Andrade-Watkins, (Cambridge, Mass.: MIT Press, 1988).
Blackwood, Maureen and June Givanni
'Black Film-Making in Europe', *Screen,* 29, no.4, (Autumn 1988), 114-118.

Crusz, Robert
'Black Cinemas, Film Theory and Dependent Knowledge', *Screen,* 26, no.3/4, (1985), 152-156.

Dhillon-Kashyap, Perminder
'Locating the Asian Experience', *Screen,* 29, no. 4, (Autumn 1988), 120-126.

Film Policy: Discussion Paper
(London: Greater London Council, Race Equality Unit, 1986).
Fung, Richard
'Eyes on Black Britain: an Interview with Isaac Julien', *Fuse,* no.48, (Winter 1987 – 1988), 25-28.
Fusco, Coco
Young, British & Black: A Monograph on the Work of Sankofa Film/Video Collective and Black Audio Film Collective, (Buffalo, NY.: Hallwalls/Contemporary Art Center, 1988).
Fyle, Chenaii A.
'Black Cinema in Britain: What Way Forward?' [interview with David Lawson, Black Audio Film Collective], *Artrage,* (September 1994), 38-39.

Gaines, Jane
'White Privilege and Looking Relations: Race and Gender in Feminist Film Theory', *Screen*, 29, no.4, (Autumn 1988), 12-27.
Givanni, June
'Black Film-Making' in *Looking Beyond the Frame: Racism, Representation and Resistance,* edited by Michelle Reeves, Jenny Hammond, (Oxford: Links 34, 1989), pp.53-58.

'IBA Censorship of "The People's Account"'
[Ceddo Film-Video Workshop], *Black Arts in London,* no.78 (16 – 30 June 1987) 2-3.
Ifriqiyah Film Collective
'Smashing the Myth of the Noble Savage', *Camerawork,* no.4 (November 1976), 8-9.
Iqbal, Razia and Simon Dove
'Mediating Asians: Interview with Navendhra Morar, Sumir Shah, Tariq Ali', *Bazaar,* no.3,
(Winter 1987), 10-11.

Julien, Isaac and Kobena Mercer
'Introduction: De Margin and De Centre', *Screen,* 29, no.4, (1988), 2-10.

Mercer, Kobena
'Diaspora Culture and the Dialogic Imagination: The Aesthetics of Black Independent Film
in Britain' in *Blackframes: Critical Perspectives on Black Independent Cinema,* edited by
Mbye B. Cham and Claire Andrade-Watkins, (Cambridge, Mass.: MIT Press, 1988), pp.50-61.
Mosam, Rukhshana
'Into the Middle of the Stream: Black Independents Aim for the Big Time', *Bazaar,* (Spring 1992),
19-21.

Phillips, Caryl
'Black and White Television', *Artrage,* no.12 (1986), 34-36.
Pines, Jim
'The Cultural Context of Black British Cinema', in *Blackframes: Critical Perspectives on Black
Independent Cinema,* edited by Mbye B. Cham and Claire Andrade-Watkins,
(Cambridge, Mass.: MIT Press, 1988), pp.26-36.
Pollard, Ingrid
'Reel to Reel: Explorations around Black Women in Film', *FAN-Feminist Art News,* 2, no. 8, (1988),
12-13.

Remote Control: Dilemmas of Black Inervention in British Film and Television
Edited by June Givanni, (London: British Film Institute, 1995).

Williamson, Judith
'Two Kinds of Otherness: Black Film and the Avant-Garde, *Screen,* 29, no.4, (Autumn 1988),
106-112 (also published in *Black Film, British Cinema,* edited by Kobena Mercer,
ICA Document 7, London: Institute of Contemporary Arts, 1988, pp.33-36).

Performance art

Herbert, Simon
'Bread and Circuses' [Mona Hatoum, and Isaac Julien], *Art & Design* [Performance Art into the 90s],
9, no.9/10, (September – October 1994), 6-35.
Hatoum, Mona
Definitions of the Term Performance Art,
(London: Greater London Council, Race Equality Unit, 1986), [unpublished paper].

Izhar, Siraj
'Respect: ICA, London', *Hybrid,* no.5, (December 1993 – March 1994), 50-51.

Jones, Dein
'Les Play Mas' [The Notting Hill Carnival], *Art & Design,* [Performance Art into the 90s'], 9, no.9/10,
(September – October 1994), II-V.

Let's Get it on: The Politics of Black Performance
Edited by Catherine Ugwu, (Seattle: Bay Press; London: Institute of Contemporary Arts, 1995).

McMillan, Michael
'A Voice in the Diaspora', *Hybrid,* no.5, (October – November 1993), 10-12.

Public art
Araeen, Rasheed
The Golden Verses: A Billboard Artwork by Rasheed Araeen in Collaboration with the Artangel Trust, (London: Artangel Trust, 1990).

BBC Billboard Project
1992: see Chronology.

Care and Control: Rear Window at Hackney Hospital...
(London: Rear Window, 1995), [partial contents: Viginia Nimarkoh and Donald Rodney].
Carlisle, Anne
'Artangel: Between God and Rambo' [with report on 'Multi-racial UK Project], *Circa,* no.38, 18-24.
'Chanting Heads, Keith Piper, Sutapa Biswas, John Carson, and Paul Gilroy'
And-Journal of Art and Art Education, no.21, (1990), 37-43.
Chanting Heads : Keith Piper
Rochdale Town Hall Square, (Rochdale: Rochdale Art Gallery; London: Artangel Trust, 1988), (publicity material).

GLC Anti-Racist Mural Project
(London: Greater London Council, Race Equality Unit, 1985).

de Schmidt, Graham
Signs of Resistance, (London: GLC Race Equality Unit, 1985) (GLC Anti-Racist Mural project: video).
Douglas, Anna
'Art or Public Art?', *Creative Camera,* no.320, (February – March 1993), 17-19.
Dyer, Richard
'Ash and Silk Wall', *Third Text,* no.26, (Spring 1994), 91-93,
(Thames Barrier Garden, London; permanent installation).

In Sight, in View: Mozaix , Black Visual Arts Poster Campaign
1990: see Chronology.

'Multi-Racial UK: An Artangel Trust Project, the Appointment of Research Worker'
Black Arts in London, no.86, (1-15 November 1987), 13.

Passing Glances: Works by 5 Artists Presented by Artangel in Collaboration with the British Library
New British Library site, London, 1990, [with Zarina Bhimji].
The Phone Box: Art in Telephone Boxes
(London: Virginia Nimarkoh/Bookworks, 1993).

New technology
Byrne, John
'Video Art Identity and the Processes of Cultural Mapping', *Variant,* no.14, (Summer 1993), 18-21.

Keen, Melanie
Out of this World: Digital Technology as a Critical Space for Cultural Politics,
(unpublished MA dissertation, Royal College of Art, London, 1995).

Piper, Keith
_ 'Fortress Europe: Tagging the Other, New Times, New Technologies', in *PhotoVideo,*
edited by Paul Wombell, (London:Rivers Oram Press, 1991), pp.112-121.
_ 'Separate Spaces: A Personal Perspective on Black Art and the New Technologies', *Variant,* no.14,
(Summer 1993), 8-11.

Regisford, Dianne
'Rapping on the Information Superhighway', *The Weekly Journal,* (7 April 1995), 5.

Art history and critical theory
Araeen, Rasheed
_ 'From Primitivism to Ethnic Arts', *Third Text,* no.1, (Autumn 1987), 6-25.
_ *History of Black Artists in Britain,* (London: Greater London Council, Race Equality Unit, 1986)
[unpublished paper].
_ 'Modernism, History and Others: Why have Non-European Artists been Invisible in Modern
Discourse?', *AICARC,* no.29 & 30, (1991), 43-47.
_ 'The Other Immigrant: The Experiences & Acheivements of AfroAsian Artist in the Metropolis',
Third Text, no. 15, (Summer 1991), 17-28.
'Art & Cultural Difference: Hybrids and Clusters'
Art & Design, 10, no. 7/8, (July – August 1995).

Bair, Vinston
Black Artists: Cultural Imperialism, (unpublished BA dissertation, Chelsea School of Art,
London, 1986).
Bhabha, Homi
_ 'Beyond the Pale: Art in the Age Of Multicultural Translation', *Kunst & Museum Journaal,* 5, no. 4,
(1994), 15-23.
_ *The Location of Culture,* (London: Routledge, 1994).

Chambers, Iain
Migrancy, Culture, Identity, (London: Routledge, 1994).
Chambers, Eddie
_ Tam Joseph, and Juginder Lamba, *Artpack: A History of Black Artists in Britain,*
(Bristol & London; Chambers & Joseph, 1988).
_ 'Beyond Ethnic Arts', *Circa,* no.21, (March-April 1985), 6-9.
_ 'Black Art', *Third World First Newsletter,* [n.d].
_ 'Black Art Now', *Third Text,* no. 15, (Summer 1991), 91-96.
_ 'On Black Art', *AN-Artists Newsletter,* (February 1985), 15.
_ 'The Marginalisation of Black Art', *Race Today Review,* (1986), 32-33.

Cooper, Emmanuel
'On Black Art', *Time Out,* (22 February – 1 March 1989), 36.

Crosby, Carol
'The Promotion of Black Culture through the Visual Arts, Black Music and the Media',
(unpublished BA dissertation, Chelsea School of Art, London, 1986).

Evans, Martin
'Third Texts: An Interview with Rasheed Araeen', *Interlink,* no.9, (October – November 1988), 24-25.

Gilroy, Paul
_ 'It Ain't Where You're from, it's Where You're at: the Dialectics of Diasporic Identification',
Third Text, no.13, (Winter 1990 – 1991), 3-16,
(reprinted in Paul Gilroy, *Small Acts*, London: Serpent's Tail, 1993, pp.120-145).
_ 'It's a Family Affair', in *Black Popular Culture: A Project by Michele Wallace,* edited by Gina Dent,
(Seattle: Bay Press, 1992), pp.303-316.
_ *Small Acts: Some Thoughts on the Politics of Black Cultures,* (London: Serpent's Tail, 1993).
_ *There Ain't No Black in the Union Jack: The Cultural Politics of Race and Nation,*
(London: Hutchinson, 1987).
Global Visions: Towards a New Internationalism in the Visual Arts
Edited by Jean Fisher, (London: Kala Press/inIVA, The Institute of International Visual Arts, 1994).

Hall, Stuart
_ 'Cultural Identity and Diaspora', in *Identity: Community, Culture, Difference,*
(London: Lawrence & Wishart, 1990), pp.222-237.
_ 'What's this "Black" in Black Popular Culture', in *Black Popular Culture:
A Project by Michele Wallace,* edited by Gina Dent, (Seattle: Bay Press, 1992), pp.21-33.

Identity: Community, Culture, Difference
Edited by Jonathan Rutherford, (London: Lawrence & Wishart, 1990).

Jantjes, Gavin
_ 'The Words About Us', *Art Libraries Journal,* 8, no.4, (Winter 1983), 14-22.
Julien, Isaac and Kobena Mercer
_ 'Race, Sexual Politics and Masculinity: A Dossier', in *Male Order: Unwrapping Masculinity,*
edited by Rowena Chapman and Jonathan Rutherford, (London: Lawrence & Wishart, 1988),
pp.97-164.

Kelman, James
_ 'John La Rose', [interview], *Variant,* no.16, (Winter – Spring 1994), 30-33.
_ 'The Caribbean Artists Movement' [book review], *Variant,* no.15, (Autumn 1993), 56-57.

Looking Beyond the Frame: Racism, Representation and Resistance
Edited by Michelle Reeves, Jenny Hammond, (Oxford: Links 34, 1989).

Maharaj, Sarat
'The Congo is Flooding the Acropolis: Art in Britain of the Immigration', *Third Text,* no. 15,
(Summer 1991), 77-90.
Mercer, Kobena
_ 'Endangered species', *Artforum,* (Summer 199), 74-7.
_ 'Welcome to the Jungle: Identity and Diversity in Postmodern Politics',
in *Identity: Community, Culture, Difference,* edited by Jonathan Rutherford,
(London: Lawrence & Wishart, 1990), pp.43-71.
_ *Welcome to the Jungle: New Positions in Black Cultural Studies,* (London: Routledge, 1994).
Mirage: Enigma's of Race and Desire
(London: Institute of Contemporary Arts/inIVA,The Institute of International Visual Arts, 1995).

Papastergiadis, Nikos
_ 'Global Visions, towards a New Internationalism in the Visual Arts', *Creative Camera,*

(February – March 1995), 43, (book review).
_ 'The Complicities of Culture', *Cornerhouse Communique, no.4*, (Manchester: Cornerhouse,1994).
Parmar, Pratibha
'Black Feminism: The Politics of Articulation', in *Identity: Community, Culture, Difference,*
edited by Jonathan Rutherford, (London: Lawrence & Wishart, 1990), pp.122-124.
Passion: Discourses on Blackwomen's Creativity,
Edited by Maud Sulter, (Hebden Bridge: Urban Fox Press, 1990).

Remaking History: Dia Art Foundation, Discussions in Contemporary Culture,
Edited by Barbara Kruger and Phil Mariani, (Seattle: Bay Press, 1989).
Rutherford, Jonathan
'The Third Space' [interview with Homi Bhabha], in *Identity: Community, Culture, Difference,*
edited by Jonathan Rutherford (London: Lawrence & Wishart,1990), pp.207-221.

Scott, Lorraine
'Passion: Discourses on Blackwomen's Creativity', *FAN- Feminist Art News,* 4, no.1, 32,
(book review).
Sealy, Mark
'Talking Hybridity: Interview with Kobena Mercer', *Creative Camera,* (February – March 1995), 16-19.
Sheikh, Ahmet
'Ethnic Arts or White Power of Definition?', *Artrage,* no.5, (Autumn 1983), 2.
Spivak, Gayatri
In Other Worlds: Essays in Cultural Politics, (London; New York: Methuen, 1987).
**'A Statement From The Elbow Room, Freedom and Change: She who Writes Herstory
Rewrites History'**
In *The Other Story,* Hayward Gallery, (London, 1989), pp.122-124.
Stephenson, Veena
'Rubbing Culture's Nose in the Mud of Politics', *FAN-Feminist Art News,* 3, no.1, (Summer 1989), 23.
Sulter, Maud
'Call and Response', *FAN-Feminist Art News*, 2, no. 8, (1988),15-17.

Tawadros, Gilane
_ 'Anthology: Welcome to the Jungle by Kobena Mercer', *Creative Camera,* (February – March 1995),43.
_ 'Black Women in Britain: A Personal and Intellectual Journey', *Third Text,* no.15, (Summer 1991), 71-76.
Tharani, Nadir
'Within the Sands: South Asian Arts in Britain', *Artrage,* no. 17, (Summer 1987), 2-3.

Waite, Lorna
'Skin Myths on the Level of the Real: Third Text, Third World Perspectives on Contemporary Art
and Culture', *Variant,* no.5 (Summer – Autumn1988), 50.
Walmsley, Anne
_ *The Caribbean Artists Movement: 1966 – 1972: A Literary and Cultural History,*
(London: New Beacon Books, 1992).
_ 'The Caribbean Artists Movement: 1967-1972', *Artrage,* no.9, (1988), 35-38.
Wood, Paul
'Priorities: *Third Text,* Issue no.1', *Artscribe International,* (May 1988), 94-95.
Wright, Mary
'A Kaleidoscope of Black Arts: Interview with Kwesi Owusu', *GLA Quarterly,* (Summer 1988), 18-19.

Young, Lola
'Towards 2000: Diversity, Identity and the Arts', in *Cultural Diversity in the Arts,*
edited by Ria Lavrijsen, (Amsterdam: Royal Tropical Institute,1993), pp.45-52.

Conferences & public debates: papers and articles

Araeen, Rasheed
_ 'Art & Black Consciousness' [First National Black Art Convention, Wolverhampton Polytechnic, Wolverhampton,1982], in *The Essential Black Art,* (London: Chisenhale Gallery, 1988), pp.36-41.
_ 'The Multinational Style' in The State of British Art: A Debate, Session 3, *Studio International,* 194, no.989, (1978), 103-105.
'Art and Immigration'
[British Art in a Century of Immigration conference, Norfolk Institute of Art & Design, Norwich, 1991], *Third Text,* Special Issue, no.15, (Summer 1991).
Auguiste, Reece
'Introduction, Aesthetics and Politics: Working on Two Fronts?', [a panel discussion with Martina Attille, Peter Gidal, Isaac Julien, Mandy Merck], *Undercut,* no.17, (Spring 1988), 31-39, [Cultural Identities conference, Commonwealth Institute, London, 1986].
Axarlis, Nick
'MAAS National Conference: A Report', *Artrage,* no.6, (Spring 1984), 26-31.

Black Art/White Institutions: A Two Day Conference
(Dursley, Gloucestershire: Prema Arts, 1987), (programme).
Black Artists/White Institutions: Conference Riverside Studios, 4 November 1985
(London: Greater London Council, Race Equality Unit, 1985).
'Black Women in the Arts Conference'
Black Arts In London, no.41, (1-15 October 1985), 12.
Brown, Gilroy
'Art is Art is Universal - So What is Black Art? A Consideration of the First National Black Art Convention', *West Midlands Art Report,* no.18.

Chambers, Eddie
'Perspectives and Directions', [Vision and Voice: Black Visual Arts conference, Birmingham: The Cave, December 1985], *AN-Artists Newsletter,* (April 1986), 14.
Cultural Diversity in the Arts: Art, Art Policies and the Facelift of Europe
Edited by Ria Lavrijsen, (Amsterdam: Royal Tropical Institute, 1993).

'Developing Black and Asian Filmmaking in London: Conference Report'
London Film and Video News, no.6, (February/March/April 1996), 1.

European Connections Seminar
13 – 16 May 1993, Birmingham UK, Final Report, edited by Ansel Wong, (European Connections,1993).

The First National Black Art Convention to Discuss the Form, Functioning and Future of Black Art
The Faculty of Art & Design, Wolverhampton Polytechnic, 1982, (conference programme).

Gandhy, Behrose
'Introduction, Questions of Language', [a panel discussion with Gillian Swanson, Carole Enahoro, Lina Gopaul, Frank Abbott], *Undercut,* no. I7, (Spring 1988), 9-18, [Cultural Identities conference, Commonwealth Institute, London, 1986].
Gilroy, Paul
'Cruciality and the Frog's Perspective: An Agenda of Difficulties for the Black Arts Movement in Britain', *Third Text,* no. 5, (Winter 1988 – 1989), 33-44, [conference paper, *Critical Difference: Race, ethnicity and culture,* John Hansard Gallery, Southampton, 1988]; see also *Art & Text,* no.32, (Autumn 1989), 106-117; and *Small Acts,* (London: Serpent's Tail, 1993).

Jantjes, Gavin
_ 'Art & Cultural Reciprocity', [East Midlands Art Conference on 12 April 1986],
in *The Essential Black Art,* (London: Chisenhale Gallery, 1988), 42-45.
_ *Black Art in a White World,* The Faculty of Art & Design, Sheffield Polytechnic,
(Sheffield, 5 March 1984).
_ 'A Conference Paper: Black Artists/White Institutions', (4 November 1985) *Artrage,* no.11,
(Winter 1985 – 1986), 3-4.
_ 'Developing an Art for Life's Sake', International Federation of Library Associations Conference,
(Nairobi, 1985).
_ 'Talk Delivered at the East Midlands Arts Conference', *Artrage,* no.15, (Winter 1986), 34-36.

MAAS National Conference: Critical Perspectives for the Development of the Non-Western Arts in Britain
Commonwealth Institute, London, 26 November 1983, (press release).
Malvern, Sue
'Art Issues: Art & Immigration' (report on British Art in a Century of Immigration conference,
Norwich Gallery, Norfolk Institute of Art & Design, 1991), *Art Monthly,* no.146, (May 1991), 28.
Mercer, Kobena
'Introduction, Sexual Identities: Questions of Difference', [a panel discussion with Gayatri Spivak,
Jacqueline Rose, Kobena Mercer and Angela McRobbie], *Undercut,* no.17, (Spring 1988), 19-30,
[Cultural Identities conference, Commonwealth Institute, London, March 1986].

Ntuli, Pitika
'Have Things Changed?: Tokenism and the Current State of Play in the Visual Arts',
[discussion with Rasheed Araeen and Gavin Jantjes], *And-Journal of Art and Education,* no.11/12,
(1987), 44-46.

OBAALA: Black Art Now
Islington Town Hall, London, 1984, (publicity material).

Prescod, Colin
'Black Artists/White Institutions' [keynote address at Black Artists/White Institutions conference,
Riverside Studios, London], *Artrage,* no.12, (Spring 1986), 32-35.

Rouch, Jean
[With] John Akomfrah and Clare Joseph, 'Culture and Representation: A Panel Discussion',
Undercut, no.17, (Spring 1988), 3-8 [Cultural Identities conference, Commonwealth Institute,
London, 1986].

'State of the Art: A Conference on Live Art and Cultural Identity'
Hybrid, no. 5, (October – November 1993), 23.

'Third Scenario: Theory and the Politics of Location'
[Midland Arts Centre, Birmingham, 1988], *Framework,* no.36, 1-68.

Solanke, Ade
_ Patricia Hilaire and Karin Woodley, 'Black Art/White Institutions Conference', *Black Arts in London,*
no.44, (15 – 30 November 1985), 3-4, (reprinted in *Artrage,* no.11, (Winter 1985), 2-3).
_ 'Pale Reflections in the Black Country', *Artrage,* no.13, (Summer 1986), 38-39,
(Report on the Black Art Conference organised by East Midlands Arts, 1986).

Vision & Voice: Black Visual Arts Conference
The Cave, (Birmingham, 3 December 1985), (publicity material).
Woodley, Karin
'After the Placebos: A Response', (Black Artists/White Institutions), *Artrage,* no.12, (Spring 1986), 38.

Arts administration and policy

'The 198 Gallery'
Artrage, no. 24, (Spring 1989), 4.
'198: Where Black Artists Get a Wider Audience'
Framing & Art, 6, no. 2, (November – December1990), 16.

'About the Action Plan: Some Responses'
Artrage, no.13, (Summer 1986), 3.
African & Asian Visual Artists Archive
(guide 1989, & press release 1995).
Alberge, Dalya
'Artists of Colour Gallery [INIVA] Redraws the Cultural Map', *The Independent,* (25 August 1992), 3.
Araeen, Rasheed and David Medalla
'Open Letter to the British Council', [correspondence], *Art Monthly,* no.24, (1979), 25.
Araeen, Rasheed
'Problems Facing Black Artists', [correspondence], *Art Monthly,* no.26, (1979), 23-24.
The Arts and Cultual Diversity Symposium Report
(London: The Arts Council, in association with the Home Office, 1989).
The Arts and Ethnic Minorities: Action Plan
(London: Arts Council of Great Britain, 1986).
'Arts Council Boycott!'
Black Arts in London, no.51, (17-30 March 1986), 3.
'Arts Council Moves'
[The African and Asian Visual Artists Project], *AN-Artists Newsletter,* (December 1988), 10.
'Arts Council's Ethnic Minority Action Plan'
Black Arts in London, no.49, (20 February – 3 March 1986), 3-4.
'Arts Council's Expenditure on Black Arts'
Black Arts in London, no.101, (1 – 15 July 1988), 6.
The Arts of Ethnic Minorities: A Reading Guide
(London: The Arts Council of Great Britain, 1986).
The Arts of Ethnic Minorities: A Role for the CRE
(London: Commission for Racial Equality, 1983).
Awojobi, Abiola
'Rich Threads in a Bleak Tapestry', [Black Art Gallery 4th anniversary], *West Indian Digest,* September 1987, 28-29.
Axarlis, Nick
_ 'Arts Council's Action Plan', *Black Arts in London,* no.50, (4 – 17 March 1986), 3.
_ 'GLAA Resignations', *Black Arts in London,* no.46, (15 December – 15 January 1986), 3-4.
_ 'Greater London Arts Black Arts Consultancy', *Black Arts in London,* no.73, (1 – 15 April 1987), 16.
_ 'Independent Enquiry Set up to Examine Institutionalised Racism At GLAA', *Black Arts in London,* no.51, (17 – 30 March 1986), 3-4.
_ 'New Horizons' [Opening of the Horizon Gallery, London], *Artrage,* no.17, (Summer 1987), 49.
_ 'Roundhouse Announces Plans', *Black Arts in London,* no.97, (1 – 15 May 1988), 4.

Baker, Walter V.
'The Arts of Ethnic Minorities: Status and Funding' [research report],

(London: Commission for Racial Equality, 1985).
Barnett, Pennina
'Artists and Racism', *AN-Artists Newsletter,* (December 1987), 24-25
'Behind the Words: The Arts Council's Plan'
Black Arts in London, no. 51, (17 – 30 March 1986), 6-8.
Bell, Andrew
'Round Pounds', [The Roundhouse], *Time Out,* (26 July – 2 August 1989), 23-25.
Biswas, Sutapa
Yorkshire Visual Arts Equal Opportunities Project, Yorkshire, 1987, (project papers).
Black and Asian Attitudes to the Arts in Birmingham: Qualitative Research Findings Report
(London: The Arts Council of Great Britain; Richmond: Harris Research Centre,1993).
'Black Arts Administration'
Black Arts in London, no.108, (1-15 November 1988), 2.
Bryan, David
'Separate and Unequal', [Arts Council's Cultural Diversity Unit], *The Insider,* (Autumn 1991), 28.

Campaign for a Popular Culture
(London: Greater London Council, 1986).
Chakrovarty, Amal
'Ethnic Aesthetics' [correspondence], *Art Monthly,* no. 9, (1980), 23-24.
Chambers, Eddie
_ 'Mainstream Capers', [Black Artists/White Institutions], *Artrage,* no.14, (Autumn 1986), 31-33, 36.
_ 'Talkback' [*African, Caribbean & South Asian Photography* by Simiola Coker and Devdan Sen],
    Creative Camera, no.5, (May 1987), 38-39.
_ 'True Colours', *Versus,* no.2, (1994), 28-29.
Concord in Devon
The Story of a County-wide Multi-Cultural Festival, (Leicester: Concord Festival Trust, 1987).
Conference on Ethnic Arts: Ethnic Minorities in London
(London: Greater London Council, 1982).

Danzker, Jo-Anne Birnie
'Organizational Apartheid', *Third Text,* no.13, (Winter 1990 – 1991), 85-95.
Davison, John
'The Battle of the Black Quotas Break Out', *The Sunday Times,* 6 March 1988, C8.
Dedi, Shakka
_ 'Black Art in Britain Today', *Arts Review,* (9 November 1984), 556-557.
_ 'Brief Background: OBAALA', *Artrage,* no. 21, (Autumn 1988), 26-27.
Dormer, Peter
_ 'Between Two Cultures' [IAUK: Indian Artists in the UK, The Barbican Centre], *Art Monthly,* no.60,
    (October 1982), 78.
_ 'Ethnic Aesthetics' [correspondence], *Art Monthly,* no. 39, (1980), 23.
_ 'Mistaken Identities' [Indian Artists Collective and the Whitechapel Art Gallery], *Art Monthly,* no.35,
    (1980), 28.

Edge, Nina
'Home International', *FAN-Feminist Art News,* 4, no.1, (1992), 18-20.
Ellis, Olwen
'Greater London Arts Association and Black Artistic Activity', *The Race Today Review,*
    (February 1986), 45.

Fisher, Mark
'Black Art: The Labour Party's Line', *Modern Painters,* 2, no.4 , (Winter 1989 – 1990), 77-78.

'Forty Years on: View from the Front Line'
[The Southall Afro-Caribbean and Asian Arts Collective], *Black Arts in London,* no.49
(20 February – 3 March 1986), 8-9.
'Funding threats'
Black Arts in London, no. 123, (1 – 31 May 1990), 2.
'Future of Black Arts in London'
Black Arts in London, no. 112, (1 – 31 March 1989), 2.

**'Global Proposals: Nikos Papastergiadis talks to Gilane Tawadros, director of the Institute
for New International Visual Arts',**
Frieze, (November – December 1994), 26-29.
Gulati, Neena
'Response to GLA's Black Arts Consultancy', *Black Arts in London,* no.76, (16 – 31 May 1987), 4.

Henriques, Julian
'Realism and the New Language' [Black Artists/White Institutions], *Artrage,* no.13,
(Summer 1987), 32-37.
Hunt, Barbara and Suzy Kerr,
'I Am Not What I Am', *Versus,* no.4, (1995), 36-37.

In the Eye of the Needle
[Report of the independent enquiry into GLA], (London: Greater London Arts Association, 1986).
'In the Eye of the Needle'
Black Arts in London, no.52, (4 – 18 April 1986), 4-5.
'INIVA in a Fix'
Art Monthly, no.174, (March 1994), 22.

Jamie, Rasaad
'Black Arts in Britain', *Art Monthly,* (March 1987), 25-26.
(Review of *The Struggle for Black Arts in Britain,* by Kwesi Owusu).
Johnson, Les
*An Analysis of Art Institutions and Funding Bodies and the Administration of the Work of Black
Visual Artists,* (London: Greater London Council, Race Equality Unit, 1986). [unpublished paper].

Kapo, Remi
'Not another Pax Brittanica: The Roundhouse under Siege', *Bazaar,* no.1, (Spring 1987), 8-9.
Khan, Naseem
_ 'Praveen Moman: L'Homme Civilise', *Bazaar,* no.18, (Autumn 1991), 26-27.
_ 'Struggle for Black Arts in Britain', *Artrage,* no.14, (Autumn 1986), 34-36
[Review of *The Struggle for Black Arts in Britain,* by Kwesi Owusu].
Khanna, Balraj
'Obscure but Important' [correspondence], *Art Monthly,* no.36, (1980), 25.

Lamba, Juginder
'South Asian Arts '93', *AN-Artists Newsletter,* (November 1991), 32-33.
'Liverpool is Home to Britain's First Black [photography] Archive'
Creative Camera, no 19, (December – January 1993), 4.
Lloyd, Errol
_ 'Black Art Gallery', *Artrage,* no.7, (Summer 1984), 30-31.
_ 'The Black Art Gallery', *GLA Quarterly,* (Summer 1986), 22-23.
_ '[The] Roundhouse', *Artrage,* no.5, (Autumn 1983), 30.

'London Arts Cuts: MAAS Condemns Arts Cuts'
Black Arts in London, no. 96, (16 – 30 April 1988), 6-7.
'London's Black Art Centre'
[The Roundhouse], *Art Monthly,* no. 86, (May 1985), 20-21.

Masterson, Piers
'India & INIVA', *Art Monthly,* no.174, (March 1994), 30.
More than Meets the Eye: A Consultative Document
(London: Greater London Arts, 1984).
Movers and Shakers: Black Arts Alliance Annual Report
(Manchester: Black Arts Alliance, 1992).

'Natural Wastage'
Black Arts in London, no.114, (1 – 31 May 1989), 2-3.
'New Committment to Ethnic Minority Arts and to Arts and Disability'
Arts Council Bulletin, no.78, (March 1986), 1-2.
'Not a Black & White Issue'
[Northern Arts Policy Development], *AN-Artists Newsletter,* (December 1988), l0.

Owusu, Kwesi
_ 'Black Art in London and the GLC: The End of an Era?', *Artrage,* no.8, (Spring 1985), 2-3.
_ 'Black Arts Centre', *Artrage,* no.8, (Spring 1985), 4.
_ 'GLAA: Racism Alleged, Three Officers Resign', *Artrage,* no.11, (Winter 1985 – 1986), 28.
_ *The Struggle for Black Arts in Britain: What Can we Consider Better than Freedom,*
(London: Comedia, 1986).

Papastergiadis, Nikos
'Imagining a New Internationalism' [interview with Sunil Gupta], *Creative Camera,* no. 327,
(April – May 1994), 18-23.

'Reclaiming the Arts: Black Experience Programme'
[GLC], *Black Arts in London,* no.49, (20 February – 3 March 1986), 10-11.
Rewcastle, Martin
'The Place of "Ethnic" in Art' [correspondence], *Art Monthly,* no.37, (1980), 17.
Rose, Cynthia
'Out of the Dark into Light' [interview with Eddie Chambers], *The Observer,* 7 October 1990, 37.
Ross, Jacob
'Post [GLC]-Abolition: the Question of Survival', *Black Arts in London,* no.47, (15 – 31 January 1986), 3.
'Roundhouse'
_ *Black Arts in London,* no.118, (1 – 30 October 1989), 2.
_ *Black Arts in London,* no.22, (1 – 31 March 1990), 2.
Ryan, Marie
'Interview with Artistic Director, David Bryan', [Brixton Village, London], *GLA Quarterly,* no.11,
(Winter 1987 – Spring 1988), 32.

Shaw, Phyllida
'BAC - A Multi-Racial Community Centre', *Arts Review,* (9 November 1984), 557-558.
Solanke, Adeola
_ 'Ethnic Arts Report', *First Glance,* no.6, (March 1989), 6.
_ 'Framed!: Documenting Black Visual Art', *First Glance,* no. 4, (January 1989), 5.
_ 'Housing the Black Arts', *First Glance,* no. 5, (February 1989), 6.

Sponsoring Black Arts Groups
(London:The Arts Council of Great Britain/Chiron Consulting, 1991).

Wheeler, Annie
'The Challenge of Black Arts', *AN-Artists Newsletter,* (July 1986), 22-24
[Review of *The Struggle for Black Arts in Britain,* by Kwesi Owusu].
Women in the Arts: Notions of Equality, Ideas and Observations for Discussion
(London: The Arts Council of Great Britain,1992).

Art education
Arts Education in a Multi-Cultural Society
[Draft plan for discussion], (London: Calouste Gulbenkian Foundation/Arts Council of Great Britain/
Commission for Racial Equality, 1987).

Burman, Chila Kumari
'Ask how I Feel', *FAN-Feminist Art News,* 3, no.6,16-17.

Horsford, Avril
'Access to Art and Design Education' *And-Journal of Art & Art Education,* no.15/16, 54-57.

Jantjes, Gavin
*Progress Report by the Multi-Ethnic Co-ordinator to Ian Simpson, Head of School,
St. Martin's School of Art,* (London: St. Martin's School of Art, 1985).
Jarrett, Juliette
_ 'Creative Space?: The Experience of Black Women in British Art Schools',
in *Reconstructing Womanhood, Reconstructing Feminisim,* edited by Delia Jarrett-Macauley,
(London/New York: Routledge, 1996), pp.121-136.
_ 'Survival: The Price We Pay: Black Women's Experiences in Art School', *Women's Art Magazine,*
no.38, (January – February 1991), 16.

Lawrence, Ancil
'Interview with Godfrey Brandt, Senior Education Officer at the Arts Council', *Dragon's Teeth,* no.26,
(Spring 1987), 7-8.
Liverpool AEMS (Art Education in a Multi-Racial Society)
Open Eye Gallery, Liverpool, 1990, (programme & poster).

McKenzie, Aileen
'Art as Social Action: The Art & Development Education 5-16 Project', *Dragon's Teeth,* no.26,
(Spring 1987), 9-10.
Merali, Shaheen
'An Indian Inspiration: The Creativity of Batik as an Antidote to a British Art Education',
Dragon's Teeth, no.27, (Summer 1987), 7-9.
Miles, Malcolm
'We are All in Favour of Equal Opportunities: Discuss', *Art Monthly,* no.109, (September 1987), 29-30.
'Multicultural Art'
Art Monthly, no.103, (February 1987), 21,
[First session of the Seminar in Art & Design in a Multicultural Society].

Piper, Keith and Donald Rodney
'On Theory, on Practice', *And-Journal of Art & Art Education,* no.15/16, 6-7, [Papers originally
produced for the exhibition 'The Devils Feast', held at Chelsea School of Art, London, 1987].

Pugh, Simon
'The Art British Art Schools Ignore', *And-Journal of Art & Art Education,* no.11/12, (1987), 46-47.

'Seminar-Black Art ?'
[Report on the National Seminar for Tertiary Art & Design Education in a Multi-Cultural society], *Black Arts in London,* no. 74, (12 – 26 April 1987), 2.

'Teach the Children Their Roots and Culture'
[OBAALA], *Dragon's Teeth,* no.27, (Summer 1987), 13.

Ward, Liz
'St. Martin's School of Art Library: Collection Development', *Multi-Ethnic Education Review/ILEA,* 4, no.1, (Winter – Spring 1985), 23-25.

Index:
Author, Title, Subject, Gallery